Indwelling the Forsaken Other

DISTINGUISHED DISSERTATIONS IN CHRISTIAN THEOLOGY

Other titles in the series:
The Theology of the Cross in Historical Perspective
by Anna M. Madsen

REWIRED: Exploring Religious Conversion
by Paul N. Markham

Series Foreword

We are living in a vibrant season for academic Christian theology. After a hiatus of some decades, a real flowering of excellent systematic and moral theology has emerged. This situation calls for a series that showcases the contributions of newcomers to this ongoing and lively conversation. The journal *Word & World: Theology for Christian Ministry* and the academic society Christian Theological Research Fellowship (CTRF) are happy to cosponsor this series together with our publisher Pickwick Publications (an imprint of Wipf and Stock Publishers). Both the CTRF and *Word & World* are interested in excellence in academics but also in scholarship oriented toward Christ and the Church. The volumes in this series are distinguished for their combination of academic excellence with sensitivity to the primary context of Christian learning. We are happy to present the work of these young scholars to the wider world and are grateful to Luther Seminary for the support that helped make it possible.

Alan G. Padgett
Professor of Systematic Theology
Luther Seminary

Beth Felker Jones
Assistant Professor of Theology
Wheaton College

www.ctrf.info
www.luthersem.edu/word&world

Indwelling the Forsaken Other
The Trinitarian Ethics of Jürgen Moltmann

J. Matthew Bonzo

◆PICKWICK *Publications* · Eugene, Oregon

INDWELLING THE FORSAKEN OTHER
The Trinitarian Ethics of Jürgen Moltmann

Distinguished Dissertations in Christian Theology 3

Copyright © 2009 J. Matthew Bonzo. All rights reserved. Except for brief quotations in critical publications or reviews, no part of this book may be reproduced in any manner without prior written permission from the publisher. Write: Permissions, Wipf & Stock, 199 W. 8th Ave., Suite 3, Eugene, OR 97401.

Pickwick Publications
A Division of Wipf and Stock Publishers
199 W. 8th Ave., Suite 3
Eugene, OR 97401

www.wipfandstock.com

ISBN 13: 978-1-55635-141-9

Cataloging-in-Publication data:

Bonzo, J. Matthew.

  Indwelling the forsaken other : the trinitarian ethics of Jürgen Moltmann / J. Matthew Bonzo.

  viii + 144 p. ; 23 cm. Includes bibliographical references.

  Distinguished Dissertations in Christian Theology 3

  ISBN 13: 978-1-55635-141-9

  1. Moltmann, Jürgen. 2. Christian ethics. 3. Hope—Religious aspects—Christianity. 4. Christian life. I. Title. II. Series.

BV4638 B66 2009

Manufactured in the U.S.A.

Contents

Acknowledgements vii
Abbreviations of Frequently Cited Works by Moltmann viii

Introduction 1

CHAPTER 1
Hope for the World
Copying God 3

CHAPTER 2
Mutual *Perichoresis*
From Divine Apathy to Divine Passion 22

CHAPTER 3
Divine Love
Philia and Agape 36

CHAPTER 4
Jesus Christ as Cosmic Linchpin
Identity in Infinite Contradiction 52

CHAPTER 5
The Sabbath Feast of Redemption
Cosmic Perichoresis 69

CHAPTER 6
The Ethics of Discipleship
Fellowship in the Trinity 83

CHAPTER 7
The Ethics of Ambiguity
Self-Sacrifice and Self-Assertion 111

Bibliography 131

Acknowledgements

To Prof. James Olthuis whose patience, insight, and encouragement have been with me every step of this long journey. To call him mentor and friend is a privilege.

To my co-promoter, Prof. Aad van Egmond of Vrije Universiteit, Amsterdam, whose willingness to work through my many drafts and offer his expertise has deepened my understanding and encouraged me along the way.

To the members of my dissertation committee whose suggestions have strengthened this work.

To Jürgen Moltmann for his creativity, insight, and faithfulness, and his willingness to spend time with yet another student.

To the faculty of the Institute for Christian Studies who have shaped my life and work, especially Hendrik Hart and Calvin Seerveld.

To the intellectual and spiritual community of the Institute for Christian Studies whose members have blessed me from near and far.

To Kathleen Kennedy for her close reading of several chapters.

To my colleagues at Cornerstone University who have been with me, especially Michael Stevens, Randall Burghart, Tim Detwiler, Mike Cuffman, and Matt Zainea.

To my students at Cornerstone University who have challenged me inside and outside the classroom, especially Larry Baker, Luke Moord, Brad Wortz, John Monda, Matt Harrison and Chris Allers.

To my sisters and extended family who have shown interest and given support over many years.

To my parents, Ronald and Bridget Bonzo, who always have, and continue to, care deeply about me.

To my wife Dorothe and son Matthias, who have been sources of joy, stability, and love in the midst of frustration and success, to whom I dedicate this volume with the deepest gratitude.

Abbreviations of Frequently Cited Works by Moltmann

CG	*The Crucified God: The Cross of Christ as the Foundation and Criticism of Christian Theology.*
COG	*The Coming of God: Christian Eschatology.*
DH	*Theologie der Hoffnung: Untersuchungen zu Begründung und zu den Konsequenzen einer christlichen Eschatologie.*
EH	*The Experiment Hope.*
GC	*God in Creation: An Ecological Doctrine of Creation.*
HTG	*History and the Triune God: Contributions to Trinitarian Theology.*
SL	*The Spirit of Life: A Universal Affirmation.*
TH	*Theology of Hope: On the Ground and the Implications of a Christian Eschatology.*
TK	*The Trinity and the Kingdom: The Doctrine of God.*
UL	"God is Unselfish Love."
WJC	*The Way of Jesus Christ: Christology in Messianic Dimensions.*

Introduction

After the Holocaust, in an age of increasing tensions, terrorism, and violence, what does it mean to live with hope? For Jürgen Moltmann, hope is made present when the church embodies a distinctively Christian ethic and lives counter-culturally in the midst of godforsakenness. The model for the church's practice is the death and resurrection of Jesus Christ. Good Friday and Easter represent two different kinds of divine love for Moltmann. *Agape* is kenotic in character. In the sacrificial acts of Good Friday, divine love as *agape* "contradicts the contradiction" of a creation that has realized its forsakenness. But the negation of isolation, violence, and death is not enough. The fundamental relationships of creation must be (re)created.

The resurrection of Jesus Christ reveals the mutual indwelling of the God the Father, Son, and Spirit. The community manifest in the life of the Trinity is characterized by *philia*. *Philia* is a love which seeks deeper and deeper connections amongst its members and produces an abiding unity. The *perichoresis* experienced in inner-trinitarian life becomes the end for all of reality. Creation finds fulfillment as part of divine life. Divine love as *agape* has overcome any distance between God and creation and reconciles creation into the reciprocal relationships of divine *philia*. The church's call, as those who have experienced this reconciliation, is to offer the hope of the *philia* of divine life to a hopeless world by acting in *agape* towards those who (violently) oppose God.

This study is a critical reading of Jürgen Moltmann's ethics of discipleship. His turn to the inner life of the Trinity as his source for his reflections on the life of the church is not without problems. While the call to copy God in our relationships offers some general direction for our actions, it also raises several questions. Two important questions for this work are, "In what way are we to copy God?" and "What conditions make it possible to copy God?" In the end, I will argue, Moltmann's answers to these questions are insufficient; and, consequently, he fails to protect the difference between Creator and creation in his *analogia relationis*. As a result, the ethical direction given by Moltmann's work seems to be increasingly muddied and, at best, paradoxical.

In a world of violence and hatred, how does one embody the kenotic relations of the Trinity? When faced with violence, we are to give ourselves sacrificially away to the violent other not knowing what to expect. Such a counter-cultural move is the only way to work towards the reclamation of the (violent) other.

However, for Moltmann, sometimes in the mess of daily life and its violence, we can choose to be guilty and not be sacrificial. But when? Moltmann's proposal of copying God provides, I propose, precious little detail here.

In spite of the many genuine insights and helpful critiques in Moltmann's work, in the end, attempting to locate a social program for human life within trinitarian life appears to create more problems than it solves. I will end by suggesting that we need a more radical re-thinking of the norms of human relationality in terms of God's love with which we are gifted and to which we are called.

CHAPTER 1

Hope for the World

Copying God

IF, AS WALTER LOWE has stated, "theology in [the twentieth] century was born amid the darkness of war,"¹ it would be difficult to find a person more representative of theology's struggle to emerge from this darkness than Jürgen Moltmann. The influence of his work can be traced, in part, to the fact that Moltmann's thought possesses an acute awareness of the darkness of the past century and the godforsakenness of the present. But Moltmann is not willing to leave us in the dark. In the midst of this darkness and godforsakenness, there is reason to speak of light and God's presence. It is this hope of the coming God that penetrates every part of Moltmann's theology.

In his tenacious holding to hope in the face of darkness, Moltmann "has been willing to force us theologically to imagine our world eschatologically."² Moltmann's ability to "imagine eschatologically" has presented us with vital contributions in almost every aspect of theology.³ Among the most important are his interpretations of the doctrine of the Trinity, his Christology and his understanding of the relationship between God and suffering. Throughout all his writings there are two characteristics of Moltmann's thought that are particularly striking. First, there is a remarkable consistency in his thinking. Whether he is writing about the Trinity or the problem of suffering, his eschatologically-oriented framework can

---

1. Lowe, *Theology and Difference*, 1.

2. Hauerwas, "No Enemy," 26.

3. Kearney distinguishes between desiring God onto-theologically and desiring God eschatologically in "Desire of God." This is helpful in considering Moltmann, whose use of eschatological thinking appears to be very onto-theological at times. However, I think Kearney too quickly identifies Moltmann in the line of the "eschatological notion of the possible" in *The God Who May Be*.

3

be seen as directing the development of his thought on the given topic. We will repeatedly have occasion to observe this feature.

Second, the central impulse of Moltmann's work is practical. He characterizes his work as not concerned "so much with what is always right, but more with the word which is addressed to us here and now; not so much with correct doctrine but with concrete doctrine; and therefore not so much with pure theory but with a practical theory" (*HTG* 167).[4] Thinking eschatologically is never for Moltmann empty speculation, nor is eschatology a way of escape into the future. Moltmann's pastoral concern for the church directs his approach in doing theology. Whether he is thinking about the intricacies of the doctrine of the Trinity or the proper understanding of revelation, his ultimate concern is to offer a counsel of hope for the church as the people of God.

In Moltmann's thought, the church must think eschatologically if it is to live faithfully in the godforsaken present. Only the in-breaking of the future into the forsaken now offers hope; only by experiencing the current conditions with the hopeful eyes of the future can the church find direction for living with blessing and grace. Moltmann attempts to help the church take seriously both the darkness of our age and the promise of the age to come.

As the body of Moltmann's work continues to grow, his influence continues to grow.[5] And, in the words of, Douglas Meeks, we can expect this trend to continue. Although he has already "More than any other contemporary theologian . . . provided a wealth of resources for reconceptualizing the church,"[6] Moltmann's "contributions will become all the more crucial . . . as theology turns its attention in a more concentrated way to the question of the church's faithful existence and even survival in a market society."[7]

My examination of Moltmann's thought finds resonance in his own project of helping the church to be faithful. To that end, I gratefully acknowledge Jürgen Moltmann's humility, creativity, commitment and witness as examples for my life. When I first discovered *TH*, I was, to quote

---

4. See also Moltmann and Meeks, *Hope for the Church*.

5. A helpful resource for seeing the breadth and influence of Moltmann's work is Wakefield, *Jürgen Moltmann: A Research Bibliography*.

6. Meeks, "The Future of Theology," 253.

7. Ibid. Given Volf's assertion that Moltmann is the most influential theologian in the last fifty years ("A Queen and a Beggar," ix), and Meeks' surmise that his influence on the church will grow, it becomes clear the analysis of Moltmann's practical "wealth of resources for reconceptualizing the church" is a project that must continue.

Kant, "shaken from my dogmatic slumber." The combination of passion, concern for the church, and theoretical depth captured me. Beyond his theological work, from prisoner of war, to student, to pastor, to scholar, Moltmann's life has been a wonderful witness to the hope of the Gospel. In spite of the need to be mindful of godforsakenness, Moltmann taught me to counter the awareness of the darkness of our age with the promise of God's presence. Whatever criticism I may bring against his thought in this thesis, it is important to confess that it is far outweighed by my indebtedness to the creativity and energy he has personified in his writing over the years.[8]

Introduction

The broader interest from which my thesis emerges is my concern, after Barth's critique of natural revelation[9] and the philosophical critique of foundationalism, to help shape a post-foundational ethic. After being pushed to the margins of the western Christian tradition by demythologization and modernization, the doctrine of the Trinity, surprisingly, has re-emerged as a source for re-imagining and grounding the moral life.[10] A growing number of theologians assert that the human community is called "to copy God."[11] The internal and external relationships of the Father, Son, and Spirit have become fertile ground for speculating about who we are as human persons-in-relation and for recasting a vision of a shared life.[12]

With the publication of *CG*, *TK*, and several essays, Moltmann helped re-establish the doctrine of the Trinity as a vital area for theological exploration.[13] As Volf muses, "Perhaps no single other

---

8. For an insightful overview of the people who influenced Moltmann's early career, see Cornelison, "The Reality of Hope."

9. Powell notes the connection: "Moltmann shares with Barth the opinion that the basis for our knowledge of the Trinity is Jesus Christ" (*The Trinity in German Thought*, 198). He maintains that Moltmann's modification of Barth's thought is not "anti-Barthian," but a "natural development" (ibid.). He also understands Pannenberg's work as an extension of Barth's thought (ibid., 233ff).

10. The list of contemporary theologians who have written on the Trinity is extensive, and the range of their treatments include feminist models, personalist philosophies, liberation theologies and creational approaches. The danger, which is recognized by several of these thinkers, is that Trinity simply becomes a screen upon which the theologian projects her version of what would happen in the human sphere.

11. Volf, "The Trinity," 403.

12. For an overview of the landscape of trinitarian thought, see Gunton, *The Promise of Trinitarian Theology*, chap. 1.

13. For an overview of Luther and Calvin's use of the Trinity in ethics, see Loeschen,

theologian of the second half of [the twentieth] century has shaped theology so profoundly as Jürgen Moltmann."[14] Much of that shaping has been centered in the task of envisaging the Trinity in terms of social relations. An important connection in Moltmann's work happens when he links divine social relations and human intersubjectivity. In making this important move, Moltmann grounds ethics in the very life of God.

My aim in this thesis is to explore Moltmann's contention that the Trinity provides a moral and ethical program, or what he often calls a social program for life in this world. On a philosophical/theological level, I want to investigate how Moltmann understands the life of the Trinity to be the ethical blueprint for life.

It is Moltmann's desire to develop "practical" rather than "pure" theory that sets the direction for this study. I will be asking whether his trinitarian ethics actually accomplishes what he intends. Does his theory provide practical guidance for human life? Does living according to his understanding of the Gospel guide us to experiencing fullness and meaning, authenticity and blessing in our life as creatures on this earth? Or is the ethical fall-out of Moltmann's thought far less helpful and even, sometimes, guilt-inducing?

Conditions for Imitations

In making trinitarian relations a guide for human intersubjectivity Moltmann is arguing that a proper understanding of the inner relationships of the Trinity grounds and makes available the ethical vision for being human. The foundational role the Trinity plays in showing the church how to live faithfully is evident in the adaptation of the phrase "the Trinity is our social program." Here Moltmann emphasizes that creation in general and humans in particular are, using Volf's phrase, to "copy God."

While the notion of copying God has a heritage in theology, the very idea of a creature being or acting like its Creator raises two questions: "In what way are we to copy God?" and "What conditions make it possible to copy God?" Moltmann's answer to the first question can be sketched rather

---

The Divine Community. Another important source for an introduction to contemporary trinitarian thought is the collection of essays in Schwöbel, *Trinitarian Theology Today*.

14. Volf, "A Queen and a Beggar," ix. The sheer quantity of articles, books, and dissertations published in response to the work of Jürgen Moltmann suggests the aptness of Volf's evaluation of Moltmann's influence. For an extensive bibliographic listing of the books and theses spawned by this work, see Ising, *Bibliographie Jürgen Moltmann*. See also Bauckham's bibliography in *The Theology of Jürgen Moltmann*.

easily; though much more will need to be said about the way in which he develops this position. In summary, we can say that for Moltmann divine life functions as an ideal and norm for human life; human relationships are to mirror the relationships found within the Trinity. Humans are to copy the divine relationships of inner-trinitarian life in the way they relate with one another, with creation, and with God.[15]

Moltmann sets up a sophisticated analogy, which he identifies as an *analogia relationis,* between the relations of intra-trinitarian life and the differentiated relations of human life.[16] As the analogy is fully explicated, the Trinity becomes understood as both an inviting community in which a refilled creation is called eschatologically to participate and the ethical ideal the church is called to embody in the forsaken creation of the present.[17] For Moltmann, there is an inextricable link between the being of the godhead and the ethical norms of human relationality.[18] But questions arise about this link because the intra-trinitarian life exists as the interchange between "same" Others—an exchange that is characterized by familiarity, constancy, and predictability. However, action between and among humans is not intra-human, but inter-human. Not only is there not the same kind of predictability, constancy, and reliability in human inter-subjectivity, but human relationships are further complicated by the violence of sin and evil.

Tension heightens in Moltmann's answer to the second question— what conditions must exist in order for creation to be able to copy God. As we shall see, his theology of hope begins with a radical difference between Creator and creature in terms of an initial rupture between the two. The result is that creation finds itself always already godforsaken. Without access to God, creation as a non-copy can only repeat disaster in its own relationships. The conditions for embodying divine-like relationships do not exist in the *creatio originalis.* The hope of creation comes from the promise of God to overcome the rupture.

---

15. Cunningham, in *A Genealogy of Nihilism,* offers clarity in his discussion of analogy, particularly that of Thomas.

16. The theological use of the analogy of relationality is also demonstrated by Berkouwer in *Man: The Image of God,* 72ff. Moltmann appeals to Bonhoeffer as the source for "*analogia relationis*" in *Two Studies,* 53ff. See also Jüngel, *The Doctrine of the Trinity.*

17. Gunton, in his sketch of the history of the trinitarian analogies, puts Moltmann in contrast to Augustine, for whom the human mind is the focal point of the analogy between God and humanity (*The Promise of Trinitarian Theology,* 42ff.). Moltmann's analogy is certainly more holistic in comparison.

18. See Jenson, *On Thinking the Human.*

In the revelation of Jesus Christ, divine life is available to be copied. As such, Jesus Christ is not merely the means of revelation, but also its content, as he makes visible the perichoretic relationships of the Trinity. The moral imitation of Christ is preceded by the transformation of creation from a godforsaken non-copy into an ontologically similar copy. God's inbreaking into godforsaken creation changes the conditions of the relationship between Creator and creation. The difference initially understood as rupture is redeemed in God's movement toward creation from the future. As God's presence replaces his absence, the "same" otherness of divine relationality is duplicated as creational difference. Moral imitation is possible because creaturely life becomes a replica of inner-trinitarian life.

But how does this overcoming of difference allow for the possibility of an ethic if creation is absorbed into divine life? Here I want to investigate Moltmann's trinitarian ethics by analyzing the conditions of reality that exist in the interplay between the difference/rupture of the present and the unity/overcoming of the future. In the end I will conclude that Moltmann's attempt to ground human mutuality in trinitarian life is problematic because, when all is said and done, the unity that characterizes divine mutuality trumps and brackets creational integrity and difference.

I will suggest that in Moltmann's thought ethical direction for creation comes at too high of a price. Reduced to its fundamentals, creation exists in paradox: to truly be creation it must become like God, yet in becoming like God, it ceases to be creation. God's overcoming of the rupture between creation and himself is not fully realized in history as creation still awaits the totality of God's redemption. Until that time, the difference and forsakenness of creation is held in tension with the unity and indwelling of the future. Caught between the difference of current experience and the sameness of eschatological unity, creation is called to anticipate the future by embodying *perichoresis* in all its relationships. At the point of God's arrival from the future, creation will be filled with divine life. At that time the conditions for creaturely relationships to perfectly imitate divine relationships will be met. The rupture will be healed. But this movement gives rise to some nagging questions. What remains of the difference between God and creation? Is there a danger that the differences in creation are blurred, and perhaps, eclipsed? And, like Plato in the *Timaeus*, does suggesting that creation is a divine copy taint creation with lack? Are sin and redemption to be understood as part of creation from the beginning?

Methodological Issues

My thesis is located in the current discussions of philosophical theology rather than in systematic theology proper. While the lines between these disciplines are not all that clear-cut, when I say the temper is philosophical I mean that my discussion will not focus on specific theological doctrines; for example, the doctrine of the Trinity or the doctrine of Christ. Rather, my primary concern will be to search out, trace, and explore the underlying ontological structure of Moltmann's work and the concomitant ethical impulses flowing from this theological cosmogony.

Furthermore, my chief aim is not exegetical.[19] While I acknowledge the importance of such a work for the life of faith,[20] I do not find it necessary in this present effort for two reasons. First, Moltmann's ethical insights do not rely directly upon such exegesis. Rather, they emerge from his understanding of the doctrine of the Trinity, itself more a construction than a result of exegesis.[21] Since the scriptural givens about the Trinity are rather sparse, especially about what the interior life of the Trinity may look like, exegetical work will do little to help us understand Moltmann's doctrine of the Trinity and his subsequent ethics.[22] Of course, the argument can be made that the revelation of Jesus Christ grants us insight into intra-trinitarian relationships, but any attempt to read passages regarding the life of Christ in this way would rely first on the construction of a doctrine of the Trinity which would function as an exegetical lens.[23]

---

19. A notable example of this type of work is Gilbertson, *God and History in the Book of Revelation*.

20. For example, the study of New Testament ethics in Hays, *The Moral Vision of the New Testament*, and N. T. Wright's work, such as *Jesus and the Victory of God*.

21. Gunton describes the relationship between scripture and the doctrine of the Trinity in a provocative way: "I am . . . not claiming that we can offer scriptural proof for a developed doctrine of the Trinity . . . however . . . we detect in the expressions of Christian practice in worship, proclamation, reflection, and action an underlying *proto-trinitarian depth structure*" ("Christology and Trinitarian Thought," 127).

22. The scarcity of biblical references regarding trinitarian relationships is a source for my concern that an in depth description of inner-trinitarian life is presumptuous. The issue of the limitations of theoretical thought, even theological ones, is properly a concern for philosophy. See Dooyeweerd, *A New Critique*, especially 82ff.

23. While trinitarian theology has helped to produce a "trinitarian hermeneutics," I am not aware of a movement towards "trinitarian exegesis." Or to put it another way, the current concern with trinitarian thought flows from particular issues in systematic theology and not directly from exegetical interests. While this by no means settles the legitimacy of trinitarian theology, it does suggest which issues are fundamental.

Second, Moltmann's references to scripture are used more as prooftexts for his particular philosophical position than in sustained exegetical analysis.[24] Moltmann takes statements like "God will be all in all" to be philosophical descriptions of reality and not the confessional metaphorical language of faith. While deciding upon the boundaries between confessional and theoretical articulations is difficult, I want to suggest that any time our theological knowledge is taken as comprehending and articulating a confessional mystery, we need to be wary.

As will slowly become evident, I will not be able to hide my concern about Moltmann's ability to ground a normative social program in the Trinity. Although my argumentation and approach is perhaps more philosophical than Richard Bauckham, a leading interpreter of Moltmann, I certainly share his summary description, "Moltmann is trying to hold together two rather different ideas: that (a) the life of the Trinity is an interpersonal fellowship in which we, by grace, participate, and (b) the life of the Trinity provides the prototype on which human life should be modeled."[25] And, in the end, I also share Bauckham's conclusion in doubting "whether the combination is really successful."[26]

My hesitation in accepting Moltmann's theory of the social Trinity, while affirming much of what he has to say about justice, violence and ethics in general,[27] is also strengthened because I fear that Moltmann's ruminations about the inner life of God cross into speculation or, as it is often referred to today, ontotheology.[28] There is a fine line between testifying about the Trinity as revealed by scripture and espousing an ideology rooted in a metaphysical construct.[29]

24. Plantinga suggests that Moltmann's theory of the social Trinity "sit(s) loose to Scripture" (*Trinity, Incarnation and Atonement*, 23).

25. Bauckham, "Jürgen Moltmann's *The Trinity*," 160.

26. Ibid.

27. Or as Levinas explains, "The ethical situation is a human situation, beyond human nature, in which the idea of God comes to mind" ("Ethics of the Infinite," 76).

28. See Westphal, "Overcoming Onto-theology." He warns us "to determine just where and to what degree God-talk becomes the arrogant humanism that puts God at our disposal" (161). The analogies of trinitarian theology can, at times, make God too available conceptually. See also Heidegger, "Theology and Theology" and "Overcoming Metaphysics," and Caputo, *Demythologizing Heidegger*.

29. Olthuis raises the question in this manner: "What then is the nature of legitimate theologizing about the Trinity, and when is the boundary to metaphysics or ontotheology crossed. That is a complex question . . ." (Olthuis, "A Radical Ontology"). He chooses to emphasis the kingdom of God as a point of departure for theorizing about the moral life, in contrast to the inner life of the Trinity. Marion warns that "to do theology is not to speak the language of the gods or 'God'" (*God Without Being*, 143).

Divergent Readings

Any work—including this one—that seeks to deepen our insight into Moltmann's overarching ontological structure or theological cosmogony faces the reality that interpreters are far from one mind in describing his fundamental position. There is no disagreement about the fact that for Moltmann the eschatological hope of life in/with the Trinity is set in opposition to the despair of godforsaken existence. The differences arise where some argue that Moltmann stresses the discontinuity between the God-filled future and the godforsaken present, while others see him highlighting the continuity.

The emphasis on the future as God's dwelling place led, it is said, to a denial of any experience of God in the present as the divide between God and creation was seen as intrinsic to creation being creation.[30] Early critics asserted that creation and new creation are so discontinuous in Moltmann that any continuity of creation into the eschaton is impossible; therefore, *creatio originalis* is void of meaning.

In Langdon Gilkey's early reading of *TH*, the openness that results from creation's kenosis is necessary because of the lack of any presence in creation. In creation's kenosis, creation is merely emptying itself of that which does not belong, which is everything. The absolute disjuncture between the future and the present undercuts any notion of continuity. In Gilkey's assessment, Moltmann's God of the future negates and violates creation. Far from being a "turning to the world," Gilkey alleges that in Moltmann "the divine presence . . . is the negation of the world in the cross."[31] Gilkey further explains that in Moltmann there is a "radical denial of the importance of the doctrines of God's present activity through creation, and so of the relevance of culture, secular or otherwise, to theology and our understanding of God."[32]

While for Gilkey "eschatology depends . . . on a positive relation of faith to present culture, and thus on an understanding of the activity of God in the present *saeculum*,"[33] for Moltmann it is history that ultimately depends on eschatology. That which can be "experienced, remembered, and expected as 'history' is set and filled, revealed and fashioned, by promise"

---

30. See Bauckham, *The Theology of Jürgen Moltmann*, 23ff. Early critics viewed *TH* as a horizontalized version of Barth's dualism that maintained the rupture between revelation and experience. See also Meeks, *Origins*, 16–19, and Bauckham, *Moltmann: Messianic Theology*, 5.

31. Gilkey, "The Contribution of Culture," 36.

32. Ibid.

33. Ibid., 39.

(*TH* 106). Gilkey's criticism addresses the contingent character of human history. The presence of God stands over against the rupture of creation.

Along similar lines, the questionability of creation for Moltmann leads to serious problems in his ethics, according to James Gustafson. Gustafson argues that in *TH* "the contingency of the creation rather than its orderliness is stressed . . . It is difficult to get much particular moral guidance from contingency."[34] Gustafson then reiterates and strengthens this claim, adding that there are "no significant bases theologically, historically, or naturally for the guidance of human action."[35] Gustafson understands that for Moltmann "ethics must be designed in such a way that it takes into account historical changes and the processes by which moral choices are made."[36] Yet, Gustafson argues, there must be some continuity or stability in the principles that guide this process. Moltmann acknowledges this need, but it is "only in terms of a concrete future (that) ethical instants acquire continuity."[37] This move does not solve the problem for Gustafson because this concrete future "is simply and only a relativization of all present things."[38] The result is that Moltmann's ethic of kenosis ends up producing only an "empty openness."[39] Gustafson believes that in the end Moltmann can only tell us that "things are not immutable; they can be changed. God, the future, makes possible hope and courage."[40]

As Moltmann's primary concern is for a practical theory, Gustafson's critique, if on track, would be very disconcerting. If Moltmann's thought offers little more than a rejection of the forsaken here and now, the moral direction of his theory would be difficult to uncover. In this reading, the necessity of creation's rupture to provide the opening for God's presence in Moltmann is a devaluation of creation. The anticipation by creation for the filling of the openness with the kingdom of God is illusory because the eschaton has been robbed of all its meaning in creation's negation. The negation of creation leads to a denial of God's presence in creation and the loss of any positive role for ethics. In Moltmann's thought, the emptying of creation to make room for the coming of creation's Other is understood by Gilkey and Gustafson to be an abandonment of creation.

---

34. Gustafson, *Theology and Ethics*, 45.
35. Ibid., 48.
36. Ibid., 46.
37. Ibid., 47.
38. Ibid.
39. *Hope and Planning*, 122.
40. Gustafson, *Theology and Ethics*, 48.

The overwhelming presence of God in the future does not compensate for his absence from the present.

Contrary to Gilkey's and Gustafson's readings of the eschatological openness of *TH* is the emphasis Douglas Meeks places on Moltmann's understanding of the forsakenness of creation as a necessary step in a real process of reconciliation. In arguing that the doctrine of reconciliation is foundational to the theology of hope, Meeks counters Gilkey and Gustafson by holding that there is continuity within the discontinuity for Moltmann. Meeks sees Moltmann as pointing to the work of Christ as creating a space in which intimacy between God and creation can be established. Meeks asserts that "(h)ope, eschatology, promise, the future, the resurrection, the cross: from any particular perspective any one of these subjects might be considered the comprehensive designation of or the undeniable key to the theology of hope. None, however, is more than a crucial component of the overall dialectic of reconciliation."[41] Meeks maintains that for Moltmann "the event of the cross and resurrection creates a real process of reconciliation. Thus history . . . will be conceived as open to the coming reconciliation in the 'future of Christ' in God's kingdom."[42] The revelation of Christ confronts creation in its tendency to close itself down to the possibilities of the future. The promise of Christ opens reality to the coming of the kingdom of God.[43] The confrontation of creation by Christ means, as Bauckham asserts, "God's promise is not for *another* world, but for the new creation of *this* world" (emphasis his).[44]

When Meeks argues that "creation is good. But it is full of possibilities for becoming worse or better, destroyed or perfected,"[45] he is referring to creation's potential to be filled with its Other in intimacy or to isolate itself in narcissistic vanity. Only in remaining open can reality expect its fulfillment. The resurrection of Jesus "is not already the eschatological fulfillment of reconciliation. Rather, it points beyond itself to something not yet realized or present."[46] Jesus' resurrection is a promise to creation that it too will be redeemed from death. Meeks explains that for Moltmann "resurrection is . . . a term that has reference to the future realization of

---

41. Meeks, *Origins*, 2.
42. Ibid., 98.
43. Ibid.
44. Bauckham, *The Theology of Jürgen Moltmann*, 9.
45. Meeks, *Origins*, 115.
46. Ibid., 102.

God's creative power over nonbeing."[47] Hence, creation exists in the 'not yet' time of the present awaiting its perfection.

It is this idea that the fulfillment of creation totally arrives from the future that prompts the concern over continuity. Here Meeks sees Moltmann's position affirming "both a total distinction and a total identity between eschatology and history lead to meaninglessness and resignation."[48] In other words, the contradictory movements of differentiation and identity need to exist simultaneously. Hence, Meeks argues that for Moltmann new creation is new, but somehow *creatio originalis* continues within the newness. Meeks summarizes that reading "the visions of the new acts in terms of the old acts of God always bring to life more than was present in the old acts."[49] There was continuity within "the experience of the radical contradiction . . . because God accomplished a faithful act of identification in it."[50] Even creation's identity comes from the future. The openness of creation is the receptacle into which God "overspills" identity. However, creation itself is not lost as it empties itself of fragmentary fulfillment and opens itself to "the penetration of all things by the glory of God."[51]

Because God directs the process of reconciliation and brings identity and fulfillment to creation, Meeks does not understand *TH* to be a complete devaluation of creation. The faithfulness of God assures creation's particularity. Lyle Dabney picks up on this reading when he contends that *TH* is rooted in the later Barth's 'turn to the world,' where Barth's earlier emphasis on the disparity between God and creation is complemented with a view of "God and creature standing together in Jesus."[52]

Both Meeks and Dabney see Moltmann as turning to creation in *TH*. Both hold that in Moltmann's view of reconciliation Christ does not reestablish some line of continuity of being between God and creation.[53]

47. Ibid., 98.
48. Ibid., 118.
49. Ibid., 75.
50. Ibid., 78.
51. Ibid., 106.

52. "The Advent of the Spirit," 83. In a similar statement, Meeks affirms that "behind all of Moltmann's theology of hope is Barth's recovery of the reformed tradition's conception of reality in terms of covenant. According to this tradition, knowing God entails doing God's will" (*Origins*, 43).

53. Jüngel argues that Barth's discussion of God's being "takes place doubtless in the Christology of the *Church Dogmatics*, which therefore on this account not only determines the whole *Dogmatics* but accompanies it in the form of fundamental paragraphs. That part of the *Church Dogmatics* which especially deals with Christology is the doctrine of reconciliation" (*The Doctrine of the Trinity*, 1). Lowe contends that it is ethics' problematic

The person of faith must accept the promise of God's coming presence and live in anticipation of creation's renewal. Moltmann turns to creation because he affirms the necessity of creation's continuity in the new creation. Yet, this very promise of the future perfection of creation leads to the distrust of present creation and the feeling of homelessness. As persons trust in this promise, their ties with the God-forsaken world become loosened. Hope becomes "the unquiet in the heart of man" (TH 21/*DH* 17) which protects creation's openness. In the light of the promise, human history is revealed to be transitory and provisional. As a result, "those who hope in Christ can no longer put up with reality as it is, but . . . contradict it" (TH 21/*DH* 17).

For Meeks, this means "from the point of view of faith . . . one finds the creative love of God only when he no longer creates himself out of status and achievement, but recognizes himself in the miserable of the earth."[54] The conflict between hope and bodily reality expands and broadens creation's receptivity as it awaits complete fulfillment. In understanding Moltmann's ethics as pointing to the "questionableness of the world" (TH 86/*DH* 77), neither Meeks nor Dabney view Moltmann as rejecting creation. In stressing God's desire to indwell creation, Moltmann is seen as giving new value to the cosmos. For Moltmann, creation is valued, but only for what it can become through its Other. Creation has received the promise of offspring from God.

Moltmann's ability to talk in both an affirming and a rejecting way about creation has led some to see a fundamental shift between his earlier stress on discontinuity in *TH* between the *creatio originalis* and *creatio nova* and his apparent emphasis on continuity is his later works. William French follows Gilkey's reading of the early Moltmann as rejecting creation, but French draws a line somewhere between the Moltmann of *TH* and the Moltmann of *GC*. In the earlier Moltmann there is a polarization "of history against nature, of eschatology against creation, christology against cosmology, and the existentialist focus on decision, act and event

---

nature in Barth which "can effect or reflect the 'great disturbance.' That is, ethics does not initiate the point of contact between God and creation. Rather, it is in the 'persistent asking of questions' and the denial of answers, that ethics for Barth maintains a tension and ambiguity. Only in a context of such questionability can ethics refer to God" (*Theology and Difference*, 137).

54. Meeks, *Origins*, 144. He also states that "for Moltmann, it is only in terms of the covenant otherness of God that man becomes aware of the profound misery in himself and his world" (*Origins*, 153).

against metaphysics and natural law."⁵⁵ The result of this radical distinction between present and future has "led to destructive distortions of our notions about God's action in the world, the status of creation and our theological picture of the human person."⁵⁶ In his review of *GC*, French argues that when it is "read against Moltmann's earlier works, this book displays a grand reversal of theological direction and sensibility, a seismic shift from a focus on history, eschatology, and 'openness to the future' to one on nature, creation, and respect for 'dwelling' within the present."⁵⁷

French highlights the change he sees in Moltmann by contrasting passages from earlier works and *GC*: "Where once he challenged us not to live in 'the world' as our 'home,' Moltmann now in *God in Creation* shifts direction to hold that the 'messianic promise' is that 'the world should be home.'"⁵⁸ While holding in *TH* that "'all reality' is 'inadequate' and 'surpassable'" and describing "the world as 'Godless,' and reality as 'corrupt,'"⁵⁹ later in *GC* Moltmann argues that "human history 'must be brought into harmony with the laws of life and the rhythm of nature.'"⁶⁰ French concludes that in spite of "deep continuities" there is a "great sea of change that separates *God in Creation* from Moltmann's earlier agenda."⁶¹ In fact the sea of change is so great that French brings his analysis to a climax with his claim that "if Moltmann is right now, he was wrong then."⁶² Moltmann has substituted a new creation-friendly cosmogony for the old cosmogony that devalued creation.

To follow French's reading we would essentially have to say that there are two distinct positions in Moltmann's work, separated by a "great sea of change." But such a reading, we will argue, fails to account for the underlying consistency throughout his entire corpus of central themes, first developed in *TH*. Even if there may be something to the criticism that Moltmann lacks "philosophical analysis and logical rigor,"⁶³ which could easily lead to possible confusions, opting for French's "seismic shift" in Moltmann fails to recognize the consistency by which Moltmann employs oppositional

55. French, "Returning to Creation," 78. See also Mortensen, "Schöpfungstheologie und Anthropologie," 466–72, and Hafstad, "Gott in der Natur," 460–65.
56. Ibid.
57. Ibid., 79.
58. Ibid., 80.
59. Ibid., 81.
60. Ibid.
61. Ibid.
62. Ibid., 78.
63. Bauckham, "Jürgen Moltmann," 308.

pairs to capture the dynamic nature of reality. These oppositional pairs—or themes in "radical contradiction" as Meeks describes—represent an essential differentiation of reality, but a differentiation that, at the same time, exhibits both an originary and consummatory unity. So while Moltmann may at times, for example, emphasize *philia* (love of like for like) over *agape* (love for the different) or divine absence over divine presence or *creatio nova* over *creatio originalis*, such points of emphasis do not in the least deny that both *philia* and *agape* are, however contradictory, movements of a single divine love. In this reading, I differ from McDougall's recent interpretation of Moltmann's view of love. She pays little attention to *philia* and instead focuses on *agape* as "the biblical principle of love."[64] She is more concerned with the distinction of "creative love" and "crucified love" in Moltmann's conception of *agape*. In so doing, she under-emphasizes the dialectical structure of Moltmann's thought.

In contrast, Richard Bauckham (as well as Meeks) does acknowledge the play between opposites when he asserts, "apparent major changes of direction in Moltmann usually turn out, on closer study of his work, to be deeply rooted in an essentially continuous development of his thought."[65] Moltmann himself talks about his work in this way. While he readily acknowledges the tension between early and later works and even within a given work, he certainly does not understand any shift in emphasis to be a radical departure from his theology of hope.[66] Nowhere does Moltmann admit to departing from a theology of hope. Moltmann views any shift in focus as necessary in his attempt to adequately describe the nature of reality. For example, he explains that the shift from *TH*'s emphasis on the forsakenness of creation to *GC*'s emphasis on creation as home is necessary because "always to stress only the distinction between God and the world in the doctrine of creation is to adopt a one-sided approach . . ." (*HTG* 133).[67]

64. McDougall, *Pilgrimage of Love*, 44.

65. Bauckham, *The Theology of Jürgen Moltmann*, 214.

66. See Moltmann's reflection in *HTG* on his theological career, in which he declares, "I did not attempt to write these books as theological textbooks, informative on all sides, balanced in judgment and reassuring in wisdom. In them I wanted to say something specific in a particular cultural, theological and political situation, and took sides" (173). As stated in the introduction of this work, Moltmann considers his work in three phases, not as three separate theologies. The wide range of topics and conversational partners results in different emphases. Some inconsistency, or lack of rigor, results because, to use Rorty's distinction, Moltmann is a 'world-revealer' and not a 'problem-solver.'

67. Dabney picks up on this reading when he contends that *TH* is rooted in the later Barth's 'turn to the world,' where Barth's earlier emphasis on the disparity between God

Contradictory Monism

My own take on this state of affairs is that it is a unique trait of Moltmann's position that he simultaneously stresses both continuity and discontinuity. As Meeks—, I believe rightly—noted, Moltmann believes that emphasizing both "total distinction and total identity between eschatology and history lead to meaninglessness and resignation."[68] Rather both the distinction of discontinuity and the continuity of identity need to be held on to in and through their contradiction. It is this simultaneous opposition and harmony—unity in opposition—that is the characterizing and integrating feature of Moltmann's cosmogony. For Moltmann the reality of the cosmos is inherently contradictory. Indeed, I want to suggest that Moltmann's complex thought especially comes into coherent and fruitful focus when it is seen as a cosmic coincidence of opposites, a position that in this thesis I will call "contradictory monism," following the lead of the Dutch historian of philosophy D. H. T. Vollenhoven. According to Vollenhoven, as Calvin Seerveld helpfully elaborates, "contradictory monism" (*coincidentia oppositorum*) is a type of thought that has a long history in western thought, recurring in various thinkers such as Heraclitus, Cusanus, Eckart, and Hegel.[69]

In contradictory monism reality is, as James Olthuis explains, caught up in "the cosmic process (that) is inherently contradictory and eternally recurring."[70] There are two horizontal currents continually and eternally occurring. The movements concurrently run counter as "the universal cosmic law realizes itself in a process of differentiation" even as "there is the process in the opposite direction of a return to the universal origin and unity."[71] In contradictory/harmonic monism, the direction of differentiation is usually considered to be "the direction of time, of immediate experience, and of ordinary life."[72] The originary unity mutates into a plurality within temporal reality. The dynamic processes of time result in the differentiation of the universal into the particulars. The second con-

---

and creation is complemented with a view of "God and creature standing together in Jesus" ("Advent," 83).

68. Meeks, *Origins*, 118.

69. For a helpful presentation of contradictory monism understood historically, see Seerveld, "Biblical Wisdom," 127–43. In understanding Moltmann through these categories I am following the work of Walsh in "Theology of Hope" and his review of *The Trinity and the Kingdom of God*.

70. Olthuis, *Models of Humankind*, 29.

71. Ibid.

72. Ibid.

current movement is towards unity. In this direction, the experience is of the "wholly other, of a different direction, eternal, trans-personal and sacred."[73] The direction of the eternal manifests the originary and ultimate unity that makes this position monistic. When the movement of unity is revealed within differentiated reality "ordinary human experience becomes something else, divine, yet it remains itself."[74] The issue at hand in contradictory/harmonic monism is the relationship between the two movements. The model of reality allows for, even emphasizes, a recognition of unity and plurality and of sameness and difference; the plurality/difference exists for the sake of a greater unity/sameness.

In this work, faced with the kind of interpretive conundrums and puzzles that beset readers of Moltmann's corpus, I will set out to show how understanding Moltmann's thought (in its own unique way) as a cosmic coincidence of opposites, not only is able to help reconcile divergent readings, but positively delivers a consistent and coherent reading of his theological cosmogony. A preliminary list of opposing realities is given here as a guide to the development of our argument:

Moltmann's Coincidence of Opposites	
godforsaken present	God-filled future
creatio originalis	*creatio nova*
abandonment	fulfillment
futurum	*adventus*
sending	gathering
difference	sameness
kenosis	*theosis*
agape	*philia*

Figure 1[75]

Outline of Chapters

Consequently, chapter 2 will concentrate on explicating Moltmann's critique of classical monotheism and the various attempts to make sense of the Trinity from a starting point which (over)stresses unity and immutability. After rejecting what he calls the "god of Parmenides," Moltmann begins

73. Ibid.
74. Ibid.
75. This list is adapted from Ansell, "*The Annihilation of Hell.*" My reading of Moltmann draws upon Ansell's understanding of Moltmann's 'theocosmogony.'

to craft a relational model of God appealing to a dynamic understanding of reality which manifests itself in *perichoresis*. In chapter 3, the notion of *perichoresis* as divine love is unfolded. Moltmann, again using his ability to assert contradictory states of affairs, differentiates between two types of divine love, *philia* (love of the same) and *agape* (love of the different). This distinction allows Moltmann to stress both the safe, ongoing relations among the "same" members of the Trinity and the need for God to create a "different" other which comes to be in a forsaken place. Hence, creation is simultaneously within the perichoretic divine community and abandoned by God.

Chapters 4 and 5 examine forsaken creation's movement away from God which is concurrently God's eschatological movement towards creation and the (re)filling of creation with his presence. Chapter 4 does so by looking at Moltmann's doctrine of Jesus Christ and his take on the incarnation, crucifixion and resurrection. In the revelation of Jesus Christ, Moltmann most clearly sees the oppositional movements of reality. From the historical direction, Jesus Christ is the crucified God who displays the Hell of abandonment. From the eschatological direction, Jesus Christ is the risen Son who gives the promise of life to a creation which now lives in anticipation of God's final arrival. In chapter 5, God's arrival in creation as a cosmic *perichoresis* is scrutinized. While reality is described by two simultaneous, oppositional movements, in this chapter I argue that, in the end, he gives privilege to the unifying, eschatological movement. Problems surface as Moltmann faces difficulties in asserting that there is room for creational differences, as he had previously argued that such differences were only possible if God withdrew and thereby ceded a space within the divine community. Without an adequate account of difference the analogy between divine subjectivity and human subjectivity is severely weakened.

Chapter 6 is concerned with the ethical implications drawn from intra-trinitarian life. Moltmann's understanding of the church's call to witness through an anticipatory, self-sacrificing, non-violent life is rooted in his model of God, his view of creation, and the (dis)connection between them. However, his ethic allows for the possibility of self-assertion and even violence. When and how such acts are permissible is, to say the least, ambiguous. Even more unclear is how such acts are to be reconciled with the *analogia relationis* he has worked so hard to establish.

In the final chapter I attempt to bring together the questions and concerns that have emerged throughout the study. In a world of violence and hatred, how does one embody the kenotic relations of the Trinity? When faced with violence, we are to give ourselves sacrificially away to the violent other not knowing what to expect. Such a counter-cultural move is the only way to work towards the reclamation of the (violent) other. However, for Moltmann, sometimes in the mess of daily life and its violence we can choose to be guilty and not be sacrificial. But when? Moltmann's proposal of copying God provides, I propose, precious little detail here. In spite of the many genuine insights and helpful critiques in Moltmann's work, in the end, attempting to locate a social program for human life within trinitarian life appears to create more problems than it solves.

CHAPTER 2

Mutual *Perichoresis*

From Divine Apathy to Divine Passion

JÜRGEN MOLTMANN'S "THEOLOGY OF the divine passion" (*TK* 57) is founded in John's assertion that "God is love" (1 John 4:16). "Love is self-evident for God," which means that "we have to say that the triune God loves the world with the very same love that he himself is" (*TK* 151). At the heart of the gospel of love are the sufferings and death of Christ for the reconciliation of the world. Indeed, to separate the love of God "from the event on Golgotha" is to make it "false" (*TK* 160). Christians are people who, in faith, believe in God for Christ's sake. And in so doing, they believe that "God himself is involved in the history of Christ's passion" (*TK* 21).[1]

However, as Moltmann looked at the history of Christian theology he was troubled that, in the main, "most theologians have simultaneously maintained the passion of Christ, God's Son, and the deity's essential incapacity for suffering—even though it was at the price of having to talk paradoxically about the 'sufferings of the God who cannot suffer'" (*TK* 22).[2] For Moltmann this is a startling "contradiction," an unsatisfactory contradiction that remains to this day—one he set out to remedy. "If God is incapable of suffering, then . . . God is inevitably bound to become the

---

1. Here it is evident that Moltmann is indebted to Barth, but he also argues that Barth is "not sufficiently trinitarian" (*CG* 203ff.).

2. Fiddes, in *The Creative Suffering*, identifies four major influences leading to divine suffering becoming a focal point for contemporary theology. These theological trends include reflection upon: 1) the passion of Christ, 2) the nature of divine love, 3) the problem of human suffering, and 4) viewing the world as process. Each of these is to be readily identifiable in Moltmann's work.

cold, silent and unloved heavenly power" (ibid.).[3] For "a God who cannot suffer cannot love either.[4] A God who cannot love is a dead God" (*TK* 38). To avoid such an end, Moltmann believes that "Christian theology is essentially compelled to perceive God himself in the passion of Christ, and to discover the passion of Christ in God" (*TK* 22).

In other words, Christian theology needs to start "from the axiom of God's passion" (ibid.).[5] Understanding "the scriptures as the testimony to the history of the Trinity's relations of fellowship" (*TK* 149)—"from the three Persons of the history of Christ" (ibid.)—Moltmann argues that Christian theology is called to develop a "trinitarian hermeneutics" (*TK* 19) fully and firmly founded in the life, death, and resurrection of Jesus Christ. "If one conceives of the Trinity as an event of love in the suffering and death of Jesus—and that is something which faith must do—then the Trinity is no self-contained group in heaven, but an eschatological process open for men on earth, which stems from the cross of Christ" (*CG* 249).[6]

To develop an understanding of the Trinity as an "event of love" has been—and is—the passion and genius of Moltmann's thought. In this

---

3. The rejection of God as essentially apathetic involves a significant departure from the western theological tradition for Moltmann. While the notion of a suffering God is not unknown in western thought, it has never been widely accepted. For an overview of the various theopaschitic movements in the Christian tradition, see van Egmond, *De Lijdende God*, chap. 1. It is interesting to note that two of the four movements identified by van Egmond have occurred recently; one in Britain at the turn of the century (Newmann, Maurice, McLeod Campbell and Gore) and the other in contemporary modern theology in Germany (Barth, Bonhoeffer, Sölle, Jüngel, and Moltmann). See also Sarot, "Het Lijden Van God?," 44ff.

4. Boersma, in *Violence*, has an excellent introduction to the postmodern concerns regarding God and. He examines traditional atonement theories in light of these concerns. Moltmann's work, I think, would be subject to some of the postmodern concerns regarding violence, as articulated by Derrida and Levinas, even though he moves away from the traditional atonement theories.

5. Compare with Pannenberg, *Theologie und Reich Gotte* and *Systematic Theology*, vols. 1–2, for similarities in his use of divine love as the starting point for his discussion of divine life. Jensen offers an excellent comparison and contrast between the two thinkers (*Relationality*, chap. 3). He concludes that Pannenberg understands love in ontological terms while Moltmann uses a psychological understanding.

6. Torrance, in *The Christian Doctrine of God,* has an excellent discussion on the passibility of God, in which he summarizes Moltmann's view of the active suffering of God: "In his overflowing love he allies himself with his people in their afflictions and takes them upon himself in order to reverse their suffering and redeem them from it" (248). Torrance points to a comparison with Isa. 63:9ff., but in that passage God becomes Israel's enemy as a result of Israel's rejection of the Spirit. Moltmann could make sense of this rejection by appealing to the two contradictory movements, but in this view Moltmann argues for a redemption *of* and *through* evil, not a redemption *from* evil.

chapter we will begin to lay out the general contours of Moltmann's trinitarian hermeneutics. However, to sharpen our sense of the distinctiveness and creativity of Moltmann's "social doctrine of the Trinity," it is important to attend to the historical doctrines of the Trinity that he believes need to be discarded and replaced: the "trinity of substance," and the "trinity of subject."[7]

Trinity of Substance

"The Western tradition," so judges Moltmann, "began with God's unity and then went on to ask about the trinity" (*TK* 19). This in effect is to start "from the philosophical postulate of absolute unity" (*TK* 149) which leads to considering the unity of God to be a "homogeneous substance" or an "identical subject" (*TK* 19).

This preference for unity is rooted in theology's acceptance of the pre-Socratic notion of *ousia*.[8] For Moltmann the absolute unity of *ousia* eliminates the possibility of the differentiation of ultimate reality, and without such a differentiation the doctrine of the Trinity, and with it Christology, becomes unthinkable. Another difficulty for Moltmann in depicting God as *ousia* is found in Greek monotheism's preference for actuality, which conceives the divine being as essentially static. For Moltmann, such an understanding closes down the future, resulting in the loss of hope. The inability to reconcile *ousia* with what Moltmann conceives as the biblical view of God leads him to overthrow the ontology of the actual.[9]

Greek monotheism begins with a conception of God rooted in an *analogia entis*, which Moltmann understands as placing God and humanity on a continuum of being. An analogy is developed between divine *ousia* and created *ousia*.[10] In spite of understanding both divine and non-divine realities as forms of being, divine nature is conceptualized by emphasizing

---

7. Peters, in *God as Trinity*, is especially helpful in identifying the significant issues in current trinitarian thought. See also Olson and Hall, *The Trinity*, and Coffey, *Deus Trinitas*.

8. See Gunton's discussion in *The One* of the relationship of unity and diversity, in which he offers a slightly different critique of the philosophical tradition.

9. For a postmodern critique of the idea of God as actual, see Kearney's argument in *The God Who May Be* that it may be more helpful to think of God as the possibility of the impossible. Kearney appeals to an eschatological notion of the possible. The openness he suggests towards that which should be is more ambiguous than Moltmann's guarantee of divine fulfillment. See also Marion, *God Without Being*, wherein he hesitates to think of God as Being, even a relational one.

10. Powell argues that Barth and Moltmann both reject "the speculative-analogical approach to the Trinity" (*The Trinity in German Thought*, 198).

the difference between divine being and the cosmos. By not beginning with the self-revelation of the divine being, the descriptions of divine nature found in Greek monotheism are arrived at by negating "certain characteristics of the finite cosmos" (*TK* 11). The experiences of the cosmos in terms of change and plurality are rejected as unworthy of the divine. Greek monotheism privileges an otherworldly unity and immutability. The *via negativa* of Greek thought leads to understanding the divine nature as "one, necessary, immovable, unconditional, immortal, and impassible" (ibid.).

The notion of the God given here is static. The description of the divine being is arrived at by using a negation of the cosmos. Moltmann expands what he means by calling the divine being "the god of Parmenides" (*TH* 28). The divine being is cast in terms of the present, of that which "'is' all at one and in one" (ibid.). Here in emphasizing the actuality of God, God becomes thinkable, but "non-existence, movement and change, history and future become unthinkable" (ibid.). The God who is understood as totally present is a thing "that has no past or future" (*TH* 29).[11]

Early Christianity's adoption of Greek monotheism was, at least partially, a consequence of granting natural theology a priority in describing God.[12] In this approach, first comes "general, natural theology; the special theology of revelation comes afterward" (*TK* 17).[13] When Christianity adopts this methodology, the effect is that natural theology "draws the special Christian picture of God" (ibid.). Supplementing the picture of God given by natural theology is not easy, as "natural theology's definitions of the nature of the deity quite obviously become a prison for the statements made by the theology of revelation" (ibid.).

The priority given by classical monotheism to the categories of natural theology results in "the metaphysical characteristics of the supreme substance [being] determined on the basis of the cosmological proofs of God" (ibid.). Such an effort is rooted in a privileging of sameness, so that such knowledge of God "only advances these correspondences of being to corre-

---

11. Kearney's reading of Aristotle's category of the possible is helpful here in thinking about God as other than actual (*The God Who May Be*, 83ff.).

12. Rusch, in *The Trinitarian Controversy*, examines the doctrine of the Trinity as it develops in the early church, beginning with the apostolic fathers. The tensions already present in conceiving the Trinity are evident. In a more popular way, Olson, in *The Story*, also underscores the issues around the impact of Greek thought on the Trinity.

13. LaCugna gives us a picture of the early church's struggle with these issues in her discussion Arius' view (*God for Us*, 34ff.). See also Hanby, "Desire." Augustine's view of the Trinity is much debated on the issues of unity and possibility. Hanby has a more favorable view than Gunton, who understands him to be the source of many of the problems that have plagued the doctrine of the Trinity.

spondences in knowledge" (*TK* 210). Beginning considerations of God by emphasizing connections between God and creation implies a shared participation by God and creation in the same overarching category of being or substance. According to Moltmann, in monotheism, the differentiation between God and creation only comes after the initial acknowledgment of unity. Distinguishing divine substance from created substance then makes possible the differentiation between God and creation. The consequence is that "what is divine is defined by certain characteristics of the finite cosmos, and these are marked by negation. That is the *via negativa*" (*TK* 11). The distinction is made in a manner in which it can be said "that the world is dependent on God, but that God is not dependent on the world" (*TK* 158). A metaphysical opposition is set up between God and the world in which "the world is evanescent, God is non-evanescent; the world is temporal, God is eternal; the world is passible, God is impassible; the world is dependent, God is independent" (ibid.).[14] Moltmann concludes: "it is obvious that these distinctions in the metaphysical doctrine of the two natures are derived from experience of the world, not from experience of God" (*TK* 23).

The order in approaching divine *ousia* from diverse and changing finite reality is clear: "first of all come the proof and the assurance that there

---

14. Jansen, in "Moltmann's View," discusses Moltmann's case against 'strong' immutability. Jansen concludes that "arguments for or against any version of 'strong' immutability depend on grounds other than an appeal to scripture" (300). His argument against Moltmann appears again in *Relationality*, wherein he argues that Moltmann's claim that the idea of immutability does not reflect 'the God of scripture' is not self-evident (139). Like Jansen, Morse notes in describing Moltmann's constancy that "in revelation it is not God's transcendent selfhood which is revealed but God's self-sameness in historical faithfulness was articulated in the ideas of impassibility and immutability faithfulness." (*The Logic of Promise*, 21). In classical monotheism, the very distinction necessary to maintain the difference between Creator and creature is lost if God is understood to be capable of change and suffering. Bauckham explains, "criticism of Moltmann's doctrine of God has claimed that, in rejecting the traditional doctrines of divine aseity and impassibility, he compromises the freedom of God and falls into the 'Hegelian' mistake of making world history the process by which he realizes himself" ("Jürgen Moltmann," 308). In this tradition, losing the oppositional attributes of divine substance and created substance means losing the difference between God and creator, as substance becomes homogeneous. Given such a framework, God's essentially differentiated would be a God who has fallen from the eternal realm and could not be distinguished from mutable, diverse, created substance. In attempting to define God as dynamic, it is interesting to see how the notion of unchangeability creeps back into the discussion. God is not viewed as occasionally or arbitrarily dynamic but permanently dynamic. As Lowe explains, "the banished vocabulary is thus reintroduced as clarification or supplement at the very center of the purportedly purified domain" (*Theology and Difference*, 14).

is a God and that God is one" (*TK* 17). By starting with natural theology, the characteristics of "one, necessary, immovable, unconditional, immortal, and impassible" (*TK* 11) become the prison in which divine nature must reside. As a result, Christianity is forced to build its understanding of inner-trinitarian life upon the foundation of the god of Parmenides. In this tradition, there is great difficulty, even impossibility, in moving from God as one and actual to understanding the differentiation of divine being into Father, Son, and Spirit. In allowing natural theology to define the nature of God, Christianity has uncritically accepted monotheism's inability to be essentially trinitarian. This failure yields a truncated perspective of divine life.[15]

While he acknowledges the impetus for, and even usefulness of, the early churches' adoption of monotheistic language, the concern now is for the danger Greek monotheism poses for Christianity.[16] The influence of Greek monotheism must be challenged, for "once it is introduced into the doctrine and worship of the Christian church, faith in Christ is threatened" (*TK* 131). The church needs "to see monotheism as the severest inner danger" (ibid.). The danger of monotheism for Christianity is that it "obliges us to think of God without Christ, and consequently to think of Christ without God as well" (ibid.)—and, in light of his more recent work, we could also say it obliges us to lose the Spirit.

The church's adoption of monotheism, understood in terms of *ousia*, manifests itself in the doctrine of the Trinity articulated by the early church fathers. Tertullian's classic formulation *una substantia, tres personae* has been the most influential in western thought. With the attempted synthesis of the Greek static God and the dynamic nature of the Trinity, problems arose. The unwarranted privileging of unity and actuality is the basis for Moltmann's rejection of Tertullian's formulation of God as supreme substance, as both the Son and Spirit are ultimately subordinated to the Father. Moltmann maintains that while Tertullian did argue for a trinitarian differentiation, the differentiation did not hold, as "the Father

---

15. The fear, on the other hand, of not privileging unity in concepts of God is the emergence of a tritheism. Blocher points out that "the trend toward 'social' views of the Trinity looks dangerously unaware of the gravity of tritheism" ("Immanence," 107). The charge of tritheism has been leveled against Moltmann. For example see Peters' discussion on this point in "Trinity Talk: Part I," 44–47, and *God as Trinity*, 109ff. He suggests that Moltmann's anti-monotheism may be fostering a misunderstanding that is pushing him unnecessarily toward the non-existent tritheistic camp.

16. As LaCugna points out, "Kaspar and Moltmann think that modalism or a weak theism, not latent tritheism, is the dominant danger in today's theology of God" (*God for Us*, 254).

is at the same time the whole divine substance" (*TK* 138). Moltmann interprets Tertullian as holding that "the original One would then only differentiate itself in a trinitarian sense, in order to complete and perfect itself into the All-One" (ibid.). Tertullian's position resulted in a view in which "God is only to be thought of in trinitarian terms where his creative and redemptive self-communication is concerned and not for his own sake" (ibid.).

Starting with a monotheistic conception of God means the Trinity can only be understood to be accidental to God's nature. God "as he really is" is one. The trinitarian differentiation only takes place in God's creative/redemptive relationship with creation. In Tertullian's understanding of God, as in any version of monotheism, "the category of unity prevails over the triunity" (ibid.). Western Christianity's acceptance of Tertullian's substantial formulation of the Trinity has led to Christian theology's constant struggle in differentiating between the members of the Trinity. The result is that classical Western Christianity has lifted the Father above the Son and Spirit. The inability of western Christianity to differentiate between the biblical attestations of Father, Son, and Spirit follows from this adoption of monotheism because in monotheism the divine oneness can "neither be parted nor imparted. It is ineffable" (*TK* 131).

In this case, the unity of God is thought of as "neuter, as the terms *ousia* or *substantia* suggest" (*TK* 149). However, when the unity of the three distinct persons lies in the "homogeneity of the divine substance, which is common to them all" (ibid.), there is a huge problem that leads "unintentionally, but inescapably to . . . [an] abstract monotheism" (*TK* 17). In terms of biblical testimony, the unity of the three Persons must be understood "as a *communicable* unity . . . an *open, inviting unity, capable of integration*" (*TK* 149). However, the "homogeneity of the divine substance is hardly conceivable as communicable and open for anything else, because then it would no longer be homogeneous" (*TK* 150).

For Moltmann, the problem of the homogeneity of the divine substance most poignantly shows up in the fact that it led the tradition to adopt the "axiom of God's apathy, which "exclude[s] difference, diversity, movement and suffering from the divine nature" (*TK* 21). Insoluble problems arise for Christianity when it attempts to understand the Trinity from a basis that privileges oneness, because "the strict notion of the one God makes theological christology impossible" (*TK* 131). In the strict unity of monotheism, the Son's suffering is kept from the Father's inner life. Therefore, strict monotheism must hold that the Father was not fully present with the Son on the cross.

Monotheism and the Loss of Christ

Flowing from the problem of early Christianity's overemphasis on unity and actuality is a concern about relationality. Moltmann asks the poignant question: "How can Christian faith understand Christ's passion as being the revelation of God, if the deity cannot suffer?" (*TK* 21).[17] As a result of the adoption of monotheism by Christianity, "Christ must either recede into the series of prophets, giving way to the one God, or he must disappear into the One God as one of his manifestations" (*TK* 131). In either case, the suffering of Christ is kept from the inner being of God. Monotheism prevents suffering from entering inner-trinitarian relations and thereby places indifference at the heart of divine being. Moltmann rejects this apathetic conception of God offered by classical monotheism, as it stands in contradiction to the God who is revealed through Christ in salvation history. For classical monotheism to incorporate salvation history, the cross must lead to a deep division within God and yet maintain an immutable unity. The result is the paradox that "God died the death of the Godless on the cross and yet did not die. God is dead and yet is not dead" (*CG* 244).

The problem with a Parmenidian conception of God is not only that it fails to correspond to the inner-trinitarian life of the biblical God. The failure is replicated when one attempts to speak about the relationship between God and creation in such a model. The non-relationality of the static God loses the dynamic connection between God and creation. As God becomes "thinkable," creation and its history become unthinkable. Because reality is closed down as the actuality of the divine being is stressed, "this god does not make a meaningful experience of history possible, but only the meaningful negation of history" (*TH* 29). The significance of creation, and particularly humanity, fades as God is only understood through its negation. With a static notion of God, human faith and love are "timeless acts which remove us out of time" (*TH* 30).

In the end, for Moltmann, both the biblical God and creation are lost when the God of classical monotheism fails to account for differentiation and thereby relationality. Moltmann attempts to rescue relationality for both God and creation by rejecting the notion of divine *ousia*, and the

---

17. According to Moltmann, the theology of the cross demands the conclusion that "the passion of Christ also affects God himself and becomes the Passion of God" ("Passion of Christ," 23).

analogia entis built upon it, as the starting point for a model of the biblical God.[18]

Trinity of Subject

Since Hegel, surmises Moltmann, the Trinity has been largely conceived in terms of the "absolute subject: *one subject—three modes of being*" (*TK* 17).[19] However, stressing the unity of the absolute subject leads once again "unintentionally but inescapably to . . . monotheism" (*TK* 18). For "the *sameness* and the identity of the absolute subject is not communicable either, let alone open for anything else, because it would then be charged with non-identity and difference" (*TK* 150).

Biblically speaking, this is again problematic for Moltmann. For the "absolute subject of nominalist and Idealist philosophy is . . . incapable of suffering; otherwise it would not be absolute" (*TK* 21). Once again we have an "[i]mpassible, immovable, united and self-sufficient" deity (ibid.). However, for Moltmann, only an inclusive concept of unity that is open and inviting is true to the biblical witness. The Bible reveals a suffering God who is the same "as he is in his saving revelation as he is in himself" (*TK* 151).

Moltmann's conclusion is clear: "If philosophical logic is the starting point, the enquirer proceeds from the One God," (*TK* 149) and we end with a flock of problems. "If," on the other hand, "we search for a concept of unity corresponding to the biblical testimony of the triune God, the God who unites with himself, then we must dispose with both the concept of the one substance and the concept of the identical subject" (*TK* 150).

18. Jansen concludes that in Moltmann "one philosophical understanding of God has been substituted for another" (*Relationality*, 148). Heraclitus has replaced Parmenides. This allows Moltmann to rightly highlight some aspects of God, but as Jansen points out, "the Scriptural account of God is more ambiguous than Moltmann would have it" (ibid.) See also Otto's argument in "God and History" that, if "faith means . . . to cross over the boundaries of given reality and to live in the project of hope"—that is, to transcend toward the possible—and if "the opposition of hope and experience, consciousness and being, essence and reality is always the driving force of ethical thought and historic action, then it becomes extremely difficult to see what significance God and Christ can possibly have in Moltmann's theology. Marxism has clearly propounded a philosophy of history in virtually the same terms without any use of 'God'" (383).

19. Moltmann, in *TK*, has an extended section on Barth's view of the Trinity as an example of the absolute subject. For an examination of Moltmann's critique of Barth and Christian monotheism, see Bauckham, "Jürgen Moltmann's *The Trinity*," 156ff. Willis is also helpful on this point in chapter 6 of *Theism, Atheism*. LaCugna traces the relationship between Barth and Moltmann's thought in her discussion of persons in relation (*God For Us*, 253).

Heretofore theologians have "simply added together Greek philosophy's 'apathy' axiom and the central statements of the gospel" (*TK* 22). It is time for this to stop. We need to stop making "the axiom of God's apathy our starting point," and begin instead "from the axiom of God's passion" (ibid.).

The Social Trinity

For Moltmann (along with many other recent trinitarian theologians) the concept of sociality or relationality has been embraced as a welcome alternative to a metaphysics of substance, in which God was conceived to be a solitary single individual in splendid isolation, disengaged, and incapable of suffering. In contrast to understanding the Trinity as an abstract speculative construction of the interior of a distant deity, the doctrine of the Trinity as the story of God's threeness-in-oneness is the story of God's intimate relation with creation, time, and history.[20] The cross and the resurrection are not only the supreme acts of reconciliation; they are the acts of God's self-constitution within history as triune. In summary, "[w]hat happened on the cross was an event between God and God. It was a deep division in God himself, in so far as God abandoned God and contradicted himself, and at the same time, a unity in God in so far as God was at one with God and corresponded to himself" (*CG* 244).

Love as the Giving of Oneself

The development of Moltmann's doctrine of the Trinity as an event of love is founded in the tenet that God is love. For Moltmann, exegeting the phrase "God is love" means God is "engendering *and* creative love. He communicates himself to his like and to his Other" (*TK* 59). As such, "love is the power of self-identification" and "self-differentiation" (*TK* 57). In defining love this way, Moltmann emphasizes its relational nature. Love is "the self-communication of the good. It is the power of good to go out of itself, to enter into other being, to participate in other being, and to give itself for other being" (ibid.). Love involves the donation of and by the self. Hence, "love cannot be consummated by a solitary subject" (ibid.). Love involves an exchange between self and Other, for donation involves not only the giver but also the recipient. To understand God as

---

20. Thompson notes the eschatological, and therefore dynamic, nature of God for Moltmann when he summarizes that God's becoming in Moltmann "points forward to a Trinity at the end in glorification" (*Modern Trinitarian Perspectives*, 33). See also O'Collins, *The Tripersonal God*.

love requires more than a divine self who "is" one. Rather, to be love God must be both self and Other so that the exchange of gifts can take place. The love between members of the godhead is "the *love of like for like*, not the love for one who is essentially different" (*TK* 58). This engendering love is "necessary love, not free love" (ibid.). On the other hand, love as creative goes out of itself freely to the Other who is in essence different. In this movement, "[God] communicates himself to his like *and* to his Other" (*TK* 59).

Love then implies a fundamental differentiation for Moltmann. In terms of the Trinity, the distinct personalities are not accidental to the divine being. God is to be understood in terms of relationality. God must be "the one who communicates and the communicated.... If God is love he is at once the lover, the beloved and love itself" (*TK* 57). Yet, the foundational nature of differentiation and relationality for ultimate reality does not imply a tri-theism. Sociality and personality are held in tension. In the monotheistic schema personality and sociality are viewed as polar opposites. To become social is to lose individuality and vice versa. However, Moltmann appeals to John Damascene's doctrine of *circumincessio* to develop his notion of *perichoresis* in order to describe the play between unity and differentiation, and personality and sociality.

Perichoresis

Perichoresis[21] refers to the eternal circulation between members of the Trinity that characterizes divine life. The circulation is "an exchange of energies" (*TK* 174). Love is the energy that flows in a reciprocating manner amongst Father, Son, and Spirit.[22] The exchange of energies between the three persons in inner-trinitarian life is so intense as to produce a unity in which they live in one another and dwell to such an extent that they are one.[23] Divine love is "a process of perfect and intense empathy" (*TK*

---

21. As noted by Jansen, Moltmann borrows the term *perichoresis* from John of Damascus (*Relationality*, 110). The term circumincession is used in a synonymous manner. LaCugna details the concept's use by the Cappadocians, particularly Gregory of Nyssa (*God for Us*, 72). Cyril of Alexandria called the movement "reciprocal irruption." The idea was subsequently picked up by Pseudo-Dionysus. LaCugna says the idea of *perichoresis* was an "effective defense both against tritheism and Arian subordinationism" (ibid., 270). See also Turcescu, *Gregory of Nyssa*.

22. See Grenz, *The Social God*, 43ff.

23. Powell understands Moltmann's view of personhood and "concomitant concept of love ... [as avoiding] the perils of subordinationism, tritheism, and modalism" (*The Trinity in German Thought*, 232).

175) that enables each person to dwell in the Others and be indwelt by the Others. Understanding ultimate reality as love simultaneously demands in one direction a differentiation in order for love to be given and received, while in another direction love unites by making the boundaries between the divine persons permeable. As Moltmann puts it, "the very thing that divides them becomes that which binds them together" (ibid.). Neither person nor relation is prior, but; both come into being simultaneously.[24]

The unity found in *perichoresis* is not a characteristic of a shared divine substance.[25] Such a unity would "abolish the personal differences" (ibid.).[26] "The unity of the trinitarian Persons lies in the circulation of the divine life" (ibid.), the unity must be of their tri-unity.[27] In the circulation of divine life, each member of the Trinity "fulfil[s] their relations to one another" (ibid.).[28] In the perichoretic unity, the relations are equal as "they live and are manifested in one another and through one another" (*TK* 176). In *perichoresis*, "personalism and socialism cease to be antitheses and are seen to be derived from a common foundation" (*TK* 199).

Below I have represented *perichoresis* using a diagram of contradictory monism that attempts to capture the two fundamental directions in Moltmann's thought. Here we can see both the differentiating and unifying movements. In *perichoresis* divine love is both *agape* and *philia*.

---

24. Boff maintains that "the risk of tritheism, present in this orientation, is avoided by the *perichoresis* and the eternal communion which has always existed among the persons. We should not think that the three exist, each one for himself, separated from the others and only subsequently enter into communion and perichorectic relations. Such a representation is equivocal because it considers the union as a later result and as the fruit of the communion. Rather from all eternity and without beginning the persons are intrinsically inter-related with one another. They have always co-existed and never have existed separately" (*Trinita e Societa*, 12).

25. See O'Donnell, "The Trinity as Divine Community," wherein he views Moltmann's trinitarian unity as only a moral union. This understanding of divine unity fails in its account of one divine nature. The fear is that Moltmann "dissolves" the Trinity into history.

26. Torrance describes Moltmann's position as a "tritheistic understanding of the unity," but does little to back up his claim that this "damages" Moltmann's insight into the suffering of God on the cross (*The Christian Doctrine of God*, 247).

27. For excellent overview of Moltmann's view of divine unity, see Olson, "Trinity and Eschatology." See also Aben, "Moltmann's Social Trinitarianism."

28. Dalferth argues that "Moltmann so stresses their personal agency of Father, Son, and Spirit that it becomes difficult to see how it can be said to be one and the same God" ("The Eschaological Roots," 152).

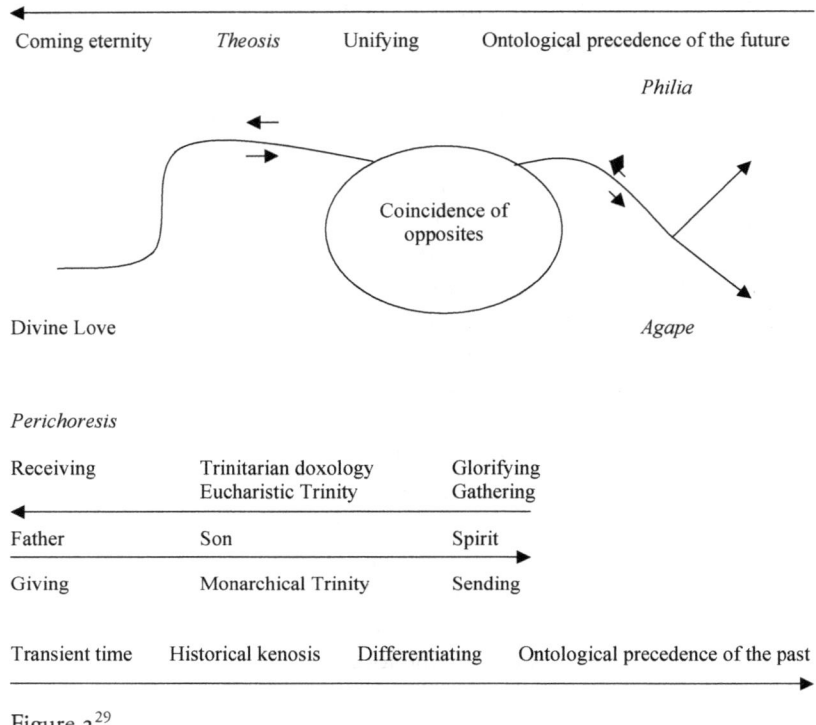

Figure 2[29]

Conclusion

The perichoretic unity of the tri-unity is what Moltmann also refers to as the social Trinity or the community of God. At its heart, the social Trinity is a different vision of reality. Rather than reducing all of reality to a static Parmenidian one that stresses actuality, reality is understood as dynamic as it is said to be both plural and unified. However, as we shall see in the next chapter, the dynamic character manifest by emphasizing the relationality of God does not yet imply openness. To understand reality in terms of openness and possibility requires the differentiation of love itself. Moltmann is concerned, as we reminded ourselves at the beginning of this chapter, that theology has contradicted itself by talking about the "sufferings of God who cannot suffer." Paradoxically, as we shall have opportunity to notice in some detail, Moltmann seeks to eliminate that contradiction by

---

29. This diagram is adapted from Nicholas Ansell, *The Annihilation of Hell*, 155. As he notes, the coincidence of opposites illustrated by the 'loop' should be 'located' at the point of bifurcation/convergence of the movements, but has been separated for visual clarity.

introducing "contradiction" into the heart of God, and consequently, into the heart of the cosmos. Indeed, since in God, "essential *self-love* must become the creative love for the Other, that is to say *selfless* love," a "contradiction or a reversal of love" (*COG* 326) is introduced into God himself.

At the same time, when we accept this fundamental contradiction or reversal in God, we make a breakthrough and do not, Moltmann argues, end up in a logical contradiction. For "it is only in a trinitarian concept of God that selfless love and divine completion can be thought together without contradiction" (ibid.).

For Moltmann, the most satisfying way of conceiving of this inherently contradictory-yet-harmonious threeness-in-oneness is to talk of the "*perichoresis* of the divine persons." In a perichoretic unity, the "at-oneness of the triune God," is either presupposed, or brought about. The "unitedness, the at-oneness, of the triunity is already given with the fellowship of the Father, the Son, and the Spirit." Furthermore, "God and the world interpenetrate each other in mutual *perichoresis*." God's "own infinity and the finitude of the world are eternally distinguished by their difference; but in this difference they are at the same time eternally united" (*COG* 327). "The indwelling of God calls into being a kind of cosmic *perichoresis* of divine and cosmic attributes" (*COG* 295). This is *perichoresis*: "mutual indwellings . . . world in God and God in the world" (*COG* 307).

CHAPTER 3

Divine Love

Philia *and* Agape

IN THIS CHAPTER THE differentiation of love is our theme. We will analyze Moltmann's concept of love as God longs for the different Other. In so doing, the differences between *philia* and *agape*[1] will be center stage. For Moltmann, "God is love" means that "[God] is in eternity this process of self-differentiation and self-identification" (*TK* 57).[2] He uses the play between the similarity and dissimilarity of *philia* with *agape* to mark the difference between these two kinds of love; and respectively, the two sets of communion. The difference between *philia*, which is characteristic of inner-trinitarian communion, and *agape*, which is characteristic of the divine-creaturely communion, is vital in establishing Moltmann's description of reality as open to the possible.[3] This is crucial because although the love in trinitarian *perichoresis* allows for a more dialectical understanding of the relationship of plurality and unity in ultimate reality, it does not yet allow for an openness that yields possibility. The permeable boundaries of Father, Son, and Spirit suggest for Moltmann a shared sameness. While

---

1. For a historical overview of the development of *agape*, particularly in the Christian tradition, see Nygren, *Agape and Eros*. He argues for *agape* as a self-less form of love. Theologians have been hesitant to use *eros* to describe divine love because it connotes need. In using *philia*, Moltmann can set up a dialectic within love, as the play between *philia* and *agape* suggests a need for otherness which is not a 'need.' Drawing upon the work of Jüngel and Brümmer, Fiddes argues in *Participating in God*, 210ff., for divine love to include *eros*/need-love. An excellent source for key writings in the (Greek) philosophical discussion of love is Soble, *Eros, Agape and Philia*.

2. For an exploration of the relationship between love and hope, see Moltmann and Moltmann-Wendell, *Love: the Foundation of Hope*.

3. Peters suggests we may have been misled by "classical ontology into assuming that absoluteness consists of unrelatedness . . . the classical philosophical understanding of absoluteness when applied to the God of the Bible will not do" (*God as Trinity*, 179).

the sameness is not predicated upon a common divine substance, there remains a predictability and fail-safeness to inner-trinitarian love as the giving and receiving by each member is obligatory. There is still no space for a real difference that allows for the possible.[4] Consequently, Moltmann's ontology of love needs more than the mutual reciprocity of same Others found in perichoretic relations to account for the dynamic nature of reality.[5] Love requires a different Other.[6]

Philia and the Divine Communion

Divine love is unified, but as it seeks to communicate the good it must "presuppose the capacity for self-differentiation" (*TK* 57).[7] The differentiation of love is evident in Moltmann's discussion of inner-trinitarian life. As early as *TH*, Moltmann had begun distinguishing between *philia* and *agape* as differing types of love. The concern in *TH* is the distinction between the hopelessness of *creatio originalis* and the promise of the future. Following his rejection of the Parmedinian God that is too present, Moltmann turns the discussion to the future as the place of possibility and hope. The source for the focus on the future is his reading of the New Testament use of "expectation" in terms of *adventus Christi* and not *praesentia Christi* (*TH* 31). The thrust of Christianity is not on seeing Christ as an "epiphany of the eternal present" (*TH* 84). Rather, the resurrected Christ is revealed as the "apocalypse of the promised future of the truth" (ibid.). The promised future, however, cannot be said to exist. Emphasis is placed on the future as possible and not actual. Hence for Moltmann, one cannot say the future *is*. Instead, the future dynamically breaks into current existence.

The play between present and future and between existence and promise gives rise to the distinction made between *philia* and *agape*. Following Aristotle, *philia* is defined as a love of the similar. But Moltmann further refines this definition by understanding *philia* to be the type of love that is directed to "the existent and the like" (*TH* 32). We can imply from the argument that *philia* as love is located in the here and now; it is the love of

---

4. For a helpful discussion on otherness and relation, see Gunton, *The Promise of Trinitarian Theology*, 171. His point that "Otherness . . . is important both for the contingency of the created order and for the freedom of the human person" questions Moltmann's use of *philia*.

5. Kristeva argues that Christian love (*agape*) is understood as disinterested love (*Tales of Love*, 139–50).

6. See also Prokes, *Mutuality*.

7. Compare with Jüngel's statement that God "alone can begin to love without any reason, and always has begun to love" (*God as the Mystery*, 327).

what is. When Moltmann places the life of the Trinity at the heart of reality in *TK*, the identification of *philia* with actuality gives him a category by which he understands the divine communion. Originally, there is God's love for himself manifest as self donation and reception. Inner-trinitarian life 'is.' Even with the movement of reciprocity between the members of the Godhead, there is still not a sense of becoming.

The differentiation of Son and Spirit from the Father results in a relationship characterized by presence, as each person exists in and for the Other. Within the Trinity, *philia* means that "in eternity and out of the very necessity of his being the Father loves the only begotten Son. He loves him with the love that both engenders and brings forth" (*TK* 58).[8] It is this generation of the Son that is the premise for the procession of the Spirit from the Father. From the inner pleasure of the Father's love (as self-communicating and desirous of receiving communication), the demarcation of the divine Origin into Father, Son, and Spirit takes place. Yet, *philia* brings forth only that which is similar in the differentiation. The nature of philia explains why "the Son is other than the Father, but not other in essence" (ibid.). Because the Spirit "has from the Father his perfect, divine existence" (*TK* 186), we can also conclude that the Spirit is other, but same in essence.

In saying that *philia* is "not the love of the other" *perichoresis* is distinguished as "not the love for one who is essentially different" (*TK* 58). While the members of the Trinity are distinct persons, they are "alike divine beings" (ibid.). The Father communicates his love to the Son and Spirit as different persons sharing the same essence. By same essence Moltmann is not referring to the participation by members of the Godhead in divine *ousia* and sharing the same actualized being. The divine essence is relational and dynamic. The divine communion is a communion of discrete persons who exist in and for their same Other. Inner-trinitarian participation in one another is the source of unity for divine life. Given his working definition of *philia* in *TH,* the natural move is to identify *philia* with the permeating love of *perichoresis*. As perichoretic, "inner-trinitarian love is the love of like for like, not love of the other" (*TK* 107).

In *philia* the self-communicating and self-donation can be portrayed as expected, even 'fail-safe.' The divine self can expect full acceptance of

---

8. Here Moltmann differs significantly from Thomas, who agrues for a strict separation of *De Deo Uno* and *De Deo Trino*. As LaCugna points out, "the net effect is that Thomas posits an intradivine self-communication that is really distinct, if not really separate from, whatever self-communication may take place in creation" (*God for Us*, 166). See also Levering, *Scripture and Metaphysics*.

his donation and a reciprocal return from his same Other. In his relational unity, each member of the Trinity exists in and for the Other. There is no room for anything but perfect acceptance and complete giving due to the permeable boundaries marking the relationships. *Perichoresis* is an eternal flow. As utterly in and for the Other, *philia* breeds a certainty and predictability in inner-trinitarian relationships. The expected reciprocity of *perichoresis* is cast in terms of necessity. Even in considering the Father as Origin of the Son and Spirit, Moltmann sees the differentiation of persons as a compulsory act, as "the Father begets and bears the Son out of the necessity of his being" (*TK* 167). Being of the same divine essence determines the Son's (and Spirit's) response, as it is "out of the very necessity of his being that the Son responds to the Father's love through his obedience" (*TK* 58). To summarize, *philia* is "necessary love, not free love" (ibid.).

As *philia*, the gifts of the Father, Son, and Spirit exist in the divine communion and are protected by the necessity of response. The relationships are failsafe. The response of the same Other to the self's gift is a given as each member's nature is essentially self-donating and self-receiving. *Philia* guarantees that each divine person will always find a receptive Other who is in and for all partners in the divine communion.

Agape and Divine Creativity

However, in Moltmann's understanding of reality, love of the like is never enough; it must become a love of the different. Divine love as only *philia* is too limiting, as "inner-trinitarian . . . is not yet creative love" (*TK* 107).[9]

For divine love to communicate itself exhaustively, it must become creative.[10] Creativity is a different movement than the begetting of other distinct divine persons by the Father as "it is only in and through its Other that love becomes creative love" (*TK* 117).[11] Creativity involves allowing a

---

9. See Jansen's discussion of Moltmann's distinctions of divine love in *Relationality*, 108ff.

10. Lacugna notes that "in order not to collapse the 'infinite qualitative distinction' between God and the world, in order not to reduce God to creation, or to treat finite creation as if it were God's love object, or merely a necessary extension or emanation of God's nature, Christians have been careful to emphasize that while the nature of God is to love in a way that issues forth in creation, still, creation is the result of divine freedom, not metaphysical necessity" (*God for Us*, 355). Moltmann argues that it is both a result of divine freedom and an ontological (of love) necessity.

11. Compare with Pannenberg, who maintains that "the coming forth of the Son from the Father is the basic fulfillment of divine love" (*Systematic Theology*, 1:429).

space within perichoretic unity for difference.[12] Counter to *philia*'s sameness and necessity, this space makes possible the realization of "God's longing for 'his Other' and for that Other's free response to the divine love" (*TK* 106).[13]

It follows from the nature of *philia* that such love cannot make free the space required for difference. *Agape* becomes the preferred term to refer to a love that makes room for the Other. Creativity finds its source in *agape*, a love for that which "is different, alien and ugly" (*CG* 28). Returning to an initial distinction in *TH*, the emphasis of the overarching argument in the book is clearly placed on giving priority to the future and its possibilities over against the here and now and its impossibilities. God's love and its openness to the future rely upon setting *agape* in tension with *philia*. The power that makes the space for creation possible is *agape*, "the magic power that brings the [non-existent] into being" (*TH* 32). This power refuses to look at the future as a continuation of the godforsaken present plagued by death and suffering. Instead, *agape* "surveys the open possibility of history" (ibid.). In distinguishing *agape* from *philia*, Moltmann defines *agape* as "love to the non-existent, love to the unlike, the unworthy, the worthless, to the lost, the transient and the dead" (ibid.).

Agape is the power to create out of nothing and the power to bring the dead to life. A vital step in differentiating *agape* is the rethinking of *creator ex nihilo* (*TH* 31). In *TH* creation out of nothing does not merely refer to the original act of creation, but also refers to God's relationship to the future. In *creatio ex nihilo*, God calls the non-existent future into existence. *Agape*'s creativity as bringing the future into existence refers predominantly to a re-creating or a redemptive, resurrecting love. While we will later return to *agape*'s role in redemption, we now turn to *agape*'s role as a description of *creatio originalis,* as found in *TK* and *GC*. In calling the result of *agape*'s first creative act *creatio originalis*, Moltmann is making a distinction that will receive much attention later. *Creatio originalis* is distinguished from *creatio nova*,[14] which is "the new creation still to

---

12. McDougall, in her argument in *Pilgrimage of Love*, 44ff., makes too much of the contrast between *philia* as "the Hellenistice concept of love" and *agape* as "the biblical principle of love." In the end, she overlooks the continuity of *philia* found within the life of the Trinity for Moltmann.

13. Highfield notes the difficulty in Moltmann's distinctions between the loves when he points out that "the world is inherent in the Father's love for the Son. And the Father's love for the Son is not free but a necessary love. If so, it seems that Moltmann has fallen into emanationism" ("Divine Self-Limitation," 65).

14. Moltmann also distinguishes *"creatio continua"* as God's continuing activity in creating (*GC* 193).

be consummated" (*GC* 193) whose movement stands in opposition to the forsaken *creatio originalis*. At the same time, *creatio nova* needs to be distinguished from the eschatological arrival of the "universal indwelling of God" (*COG* 262) in creation and the establishment of the "eternal Sabbath" (*GC* 288).

Is There Room for Original Creation?

Understanding *creatio originalis* as God's desire for an Other means that "the idea of the world is inherent in the nature of God himself from eternity" (*TK* 106).[15] Divine love was destined to transform from *philia* into *agape* because God "desires response in freedom" (*TK* 59).[16] But that does not mean there is some constraint outside of God forcing him to create. God's desire to share his love with a different Other provides the unity between the world that is passing away (original creation) and the world that is coming (new creation). Both are acts of God's creativity. Yet there is a definite logical order in reflecting upon these simultaneous, opposing acts of creation.[17]

Once the divine community has resolved to create, the necessary conditions for the creation of the different Other must be established. This move, which is the transformation of *philia* into *agape*, involves two steps: "In Act One God acts on himself, inwards, before in Act Two he goes out of himself and creates something other than himself" (CE 282). Here again Moltmann sets himself apart from classical theology, which has typically distinguished between God for himself and God for creation. In classical theology "God has an inner, self-sufficing life. Creation is an act of the triune God in his unity directed outwards"[18] (*TK* 108). The result is

---

15. For further analysis on the models of relating God to creation, see Ward, *Religion and Creation*.

16. The work of Greek Orthodox theologian John Zizioulas is important for understanding this use of love. In *Being as Communion* he argues that "love is identified with ontological freedom" (46). See also "The Doctrine of the Holy Trinity." For an interesting comparison between the Eastern tradition and Barth, see Collins, *Trinitarian Theology*.

17. Jansen surmises that "by utilizing the biblical and theological notions of God as love, the Trinity, *kenosis*, and combining them with Hegelian dialectics and modern relational thought, Moltmann has constructed a concept of God that is very different from the classical concept" (*Relationality*, 119).

18. An important article for understanding Moltmann and other trinitarian theologians' debt to Barth in discussing this problem is Molnar, "The Function of the Immanent Trinity." See also Olson, "Trinity and Eschatology," wherein he argues that the conflation of economic and immanent Trinity results in a "Trinity so open as to be threatened with loss of transcendence by being dependent upon the contingencies of history" (222).

a division between the immanent and the economic Trinity, "between the inner life of God and an act of God outwards, in creation, incarnation and redemption" (ibid.).[19]

Classical theology's stress on the separation of inner and outer reduces the inward acts of God to the justification for the outward acts. As such, there is only the unilateral flow from *philia* into *agape*. Moltmann summarizes this position by saying that "it is only as *causa sui* that God can be *causa mundi*" (ibid.). His counter to the unidirectional movement of creation begins by considering God's inward act to be more than the validation of creation's existence. There is not merely the willing of creation "outside" by God, but the taking place of an ontological transaction "in God" (*TK* 109). In moving creatively outward, God's movement is, at the same time, inwardly creative in making space for the different Other within the perichoretic unity.

Moltmann poses the question: "can the omnipotent and omnipresent God have an 'outward' aspect at all?" (*TK* 108). If the traditional division of inward and outward acts of God is maintained, "then we must assume, not only God's self-constitution in eternity, but an equally eternal non-divine or counter-divine entity, which would be 'outside'" (*TK* 109, see also *GC* 86ff.). In Moltmann's spatial understanding of divine presence, such an assumption challenges God's omnipresence. Space is understood in exclusionary terms, in which God's being in a space prohibits an Other's existence in that space and vice versa. For a realm 'outside' of God to be one in which he acts means something exists which is not God. How is this possible for an all-encompassing Being? Moltmann solves his riddle by talking about God's self-limitation. He states it as follows: "And if [because of creation out of chaos and *creatio ex nihilo*] we have to say that there is a 'within' and a 'without' for God—and that he therefore goes creatively 'out of himself,' communicating himself creatively to the one who is Other than himself—then we must after all assume a *self-limitation* of the infinite, omnipresent God, preceding his creation" (ibid.). In other words, there really is no 'without' for God, but an ontological transaction inside

---

19. Peters describes the result of this division: "What we end up with in this scheme is an eternal Son in eternal relationship to an eternal Father, rendering external the birth, teaching career, sufferings, and death of the historical Jesus. Despite sincere and authentic attempts to combat the docetic and gnostic challenges of the ancient Greco-Roman context, such Trinitarian Christologies risked sacrificing the intimate God on the altar of the beyond" (*God as Trinity*, 21).

of God. 'Without' merely refers to the space ceded within the omnipresent God for his Other.[20]

This point suggests more directly what has already been implied regarding the relationship between *philia* and *agape*. The transformation of *philia* into *agape* takes place within the exercising of *philia* by the divine communion. *Philia* is not superceded by *agape*; they are simultaneous movements of love in the Trinity. For creation as God's Other to exist, divine *philia* must concurrently flow in *perichoresis* and *agape* must creatively move 'inward' and 'outward.' The movement of God inward and then outward "is made possible and determined by the fact that 'in the depth of that life emerges the divine mystery, the inner suffering thirst of the Godhead, its inner longing for its 'Other,' which for God is capable of being the object of the highest, most boundless love" (*TK* 45).

Agape's inward movement is what Moltmann describes as a "primordial self-restriction" (*GC* 281) of God. Original creation as *creatio ex nihilo* assumes there was a time before creation existed. Relying upon a spatial understanding, the argument is that when only an omnipresent God existed reality was filled with a divine presence. *Philia* would have characterized this existence. It is this overwhelming presence of God that creates the problem of creation for Moltmann. Unless there is a difference between Creator and creature, which depends upon a space for difference, "creation cannot be conceived of at all" (*GC* 89). The first move of God in creating is making room for creation. In willing himself to be Creator, God "acts inwardly on himself" before he "issues creatively out of himself" (*GC* 86). The necessity of God's first act in creating being directed towards the perichoretic community exemplifies Moltmann's understanding of "the doctrine of creation as a doctrine of God" (*TK* 105).

The first act of creation is creating a more definitive boundary between the communion of divine persons and the communion between God and his Other/s. This boundary allows the different Other to freely respond to the gift of divine love. This act of self-restriction is described by Moltmann, following Luria's doctrine of *zimzum*, as God's withdrawal into himself.[21] It is this withdrawal "which gives that *nihil* the space in

---

20. Peters points out that Moltmann's description of 'God is love' "eliminates the need for correspondence between the immanent and economic Trinity. In fact, it comes close to eliminating the need for the immanent Trinity itself" (*God as Trinity*, 107).

21. For a helpful examination of Lakoff and Johnson's understanding of spatial metaphors to evaluate Moltmann's use of *zimzum*, see Highfield, "Divine Self-Limitation." Moltmann rejects the notion of God being *with* creation because there cannot be a shared space. Creation in its original state is competition with God for space.

which God then becomes creatively active" (*TK* 109). The withdrawal of God into himself is a "concentration and contraction" (ibid.), see also *GC* 87.), like taking in a deep breath and holding it. Through this "inversion of God" there is set "free a kind of 'mystical primordial space' into which God—issuing out of himself—can enter and in which he can manifest himself" (*TK* 110). In this space "God withdraws himself from himself to himself" (*GC* 87) so that his Other can come to be.

The coming into being of the space of God's different Other is paralleled by the perichoretic community ceasing, at least temporary, to be all in all. A new communion has emerged. God's creation of an Other is simultaneously a development of *philia* and a violation of *philia*. *Philia* may need to, as it were, transmute, or 'flip,' into *agape* in order to become creative, but "with the creation of a world which is not God, but which none the less corresponds to him, God's self-humiliation begins" (*TK* 59). In *perichoresis*, *philia* consists of a kind of reciprocity of equals. But with the presence of a different Other, instead of reciprocity we see *agape* as sacrifice: "divine kenosis which begins with the creation of the world" (*TK* 118). The consequence of the necessary limitations for God in relating to an Other that is not divine is that "creative love is always suffering love" (*TK* 59).[22] Divine humiliation is the result of the ceding of space within the perichoretic communion that it is a same Other. Hence, humiliation enters divine life prior to any response by creation. God's humiliation is simultaneous with the act of creating and communicating God-self to a different Other. For creation's response to God to be in a free space, God must first empty the space.

Creation as the Overflow of Divine Love

While creation requires a divine self-limitation and humiliation, this movement should not be understood as either coming from or producing divine insufficiency. In becoming *agape*, divine love has not ceased to be *philia*; the loves exist concurrently. Hence, while talking about creation as *agape*, Moltmann can also describe the creation of a different Other as emerging from the overflow of love from the perichoretic relationships of inner-trinitarian life.[23] In "the free, overflowing rapture of his love the eternal God goes out of himself and makes a creation" (*GC* 15). The love

---

22. See Sponheim, *Faith and the Other*, 106ff.

23. For a positive view of the relationship between trinitarian theologians and the doctrine of creation, see Bouma-Prediger, *For the Beauty of the Earth*, 120ff., and *The Greening of Theology*. See also Bracken, *The One in the Many*.

manifest by the interpenetration and indwelling among the three persons of the Trinity cannot be contained within their relationships. Creation rises not from a deficiency within the Trinity, but from the excess of love found between Father, Son, and Spirit. But the excess of *philia* must manifest itself as *agape*. Without the transformation, or "flip," of *philia* into *agape* only one communion exists and the excess of love merely circulates amongst the divine persons.

The perichoretic overflow results in "not a step 'outwards' but a step 'inwards'" (*TK* 110). At this point, divine love "is no longer addressed to the Other in the like, but to the like in the Other" (*TK* 57). The transformation of *philia* into *agape* is necessary as "like is not enough for like" (ibid.). Divine love is not satisfied with relationships among same Others. While the members of the Trinity are not identical, they are "not other in essence" (*TK* 58). A different Other—an Other of unlike essence—is needed as divine love "seeks fellowship and desires response in freedom" (*TK* 59). For inner-trinitarian love to be fulfilled it must become free and creative, as "in the love which God is already lies the energy which leads God out of himself" (*TK* 58). To not allow *philia* to differentiate into *agape* "would contradict the love which God is" (ibid.).

In *agape* there can be no expected response by God's different Other. The relationship between God and creation is not guided by necessity. Rather, freedom characterizes any interchange between them. It follows that in *agape* self-donation requires vulnerability, as rejection is a possible response to the gift. Divine vulnerability is evident in the description of creation as divine humiliation. God's self-humiliation is not only a giving up of a space within the Trinity but also a giving up of the determined reciprocity. *Agape* as "suffering love" (*TK* 59) is kenotic in nature. In the kenosis of creation "God emptied himself by virtue of his love, out of the necessity of his being, going out to 'his Other'" (*TK* 107). Inner-trinitarian love necessitates *philia* becoming *agape*, but this transformation removes creation from the familiar, counted upon responses of inner-trinitarian life. *Agape* opens possibilities.

Divine Absence and Presence

The *creator ex nihilo* empties himself in order to allow a *nihil* in which creation can come to exist. The indwelling love of inner-trinitarian life becomes a love that abandons for the sake of difference. In this movement, the *nihil* is understood not to be external to divine life, but within the divine communion. The divine withdrawal "allows creation the space for its own being," and "[i]t is only a withdrawal by God into himself that can free the space into which God can act creatively" (*GC* 86–87). The precondition of divine creativity is the yielding of an empty space within the perichoretic communion. Within this model, God remains omnipresent while within God a *nihil* allows for difference. In other words, difference calls for a harder boundary within the divine life that resists the penetration of the divine presence. Without indwelling, there is no essential unity between God and his different Other, and necessity no longer characterizes the relationship. The turn inwards is a divine act that "veils, not one that reveals" (*TK* 110). God's self-limitation and subsequent abandonment of creation into that godforsaken space are both rooted in the divine love of inner-trinitarian life, as "it is in his love for the Son that the Father determines to be the Creator of the world" (*TK* 112). Because creation flows from divine love "the world is, through his eternal will, destined for good, and is nothing other than an expression of his love" (ibid.).

God's first act of creating space within is logically followed by God going out of himself and creating the other as "the world process is . . . to be understood as a two-sided one" (*TK* 110). Once God's primordial self-restriction takes place, "God issues from himself as creator into that primal space which he had previously released . . ." (ibid.). Despite creation resulting from the overflow of divine love, it must be noted that already when Moltmann says that God "creates by letting-be, by making room, and by withdrawing himself" (*GC* 88), he is saying something about creation. The original state of creation is one of distance as God withdraws, or veils, for the sake of freedom. While in this position it can be asserted that the boundary created by God does not demand that creation, as such, is sinful, as "[t]he Creator and the creation are united first of all by his command, his injunction, his behest and his decision" (*GC* 76). It is acknowledged that creation exists in "response to the creating word; but it is not linked with that word through causality . . . there is no ontological link of this kind between the word of creation and created things" (*GC* 76–77). God's withdrawal/emptying results in a disconnection from creation for creation. Here the "space which comes into being and is set free by God's self-limitation is a literally God-forsaken space" (*GC* 87).

This divine absence does not make God responsible for the realization of evil and death.[24] His argument carefully distinguishes between the creation of the *nihil* and the actualization of the *nihil*. The space of

---

24. Schuurman reads Moltmann as rooting "suffering in the original creation" and argues that even if the fall never occurred, there would still be an incarnation and redemption from the "limitations of creation" ("Creation, Eschaton, and Ethics," 61).

creation within the divine communion space is a *nihil*, "which does not contain the negation of creaturely being (since creation is not yet existent), but which represents the partial negation of the divine Being, inasmuch as God is not yet Creator" (ibid.). Moltmann wants to refrain from saying that creation itself is evil. The forsakenness of the *nihil* exists only in potential. God's self-limitation that results in the *nihil* "does not yet have this annihilating character" (*GC* 88). Yet, as godforsaken, he does say that the space in which creation comes to be is "hell, absolute death" (*GC* 87). And, although creation's abandonment by God is not to be equated precisely with the onset of sin, it would seem to make sin and evil, if not necessary, both existentially and contingently inevitable.

At first, the *nihil* is merely a concession on the part of God necessary for an independent creation. But this limitation "implies the possibility of the annihilating Nothingness" (*GC* 88). Moltmann argues that "the stringency of the world's godforsakenness is not in itself enough to ruin it, but its ruination comes only when it abstracts the element of the expending and the death of God from the dialectical process of God and fastens on that" (*TH* 169). As God's different Other, creation is called by God's love and promised future indwelling. Godforsakenness and death become "romanticist nihilism only when they have been isolated from the dialectical process and [are] therefore no longer engaged in the movement of the process to which it belongs" (ibid.). When the *nihil* is actualized by creation's rejection of God's promise, it "acquires this menacing character through the self-isolation of created beings to which we give the name sin and Godlessness" (*GC* 88). To desire *philia* with the divine communion without fully experiencing divine *agape* removes creation from the process and isolates by closing the future that is promise. As creation disconnects itself from its creator through its rejection of the promise of its coming Messiah, these imminent possibilities of an annihilating nothingness are realized. This nothingness threatens not only creation's own being, but as internal to God, it also threatens God's being. The negative power initiated through sin overwhelms as "its negations lead into that primordial space which God freed within himself before creation" (ibid.).

The Surpassibility of Original Creation

Any self-initiated response from creation that excludes God's revealing and redeeming is premature and results in the actualization of the *nihil*. Any act by creation prior to God's contradicting of the contradiction results in a closing down of possibilities. As forsaken, creation's only hope is for *agape's* (re)creative powers to overcome the abandonment of original creation. Creation waits for God's penetrating presence. Emphasizing creation's forsakenness and its inescapable realization of the *nihil* leads Moltmann to describe original/present creation as "inadequate," "transient," and "surpassable" (*TH* 88). Original creation is "corrupt reality" (*TH* 227), which is to be understood as "a God-forsaken transient reality that is to be left behind" (*TH* 18). A creation yet to be eschatologically filled reveals the contradiction of its creator as "the temporality of earthly creation does not reflect the presence of God—it reflects his absence" (CE 284).

Creation is caught in a "transitory time" (CE 282). From its inception it is headed toward the fulfillment of the promise that it is to be overcome, and it is this promise that "constantly overspills history" (*TH* 106). The promise of the coming God "creates an interval of tension between the uttering and the redeeming of the promise" (*TH* 104). The movement in which creation opens itself by passing away is driven by the utterance of the promise. *Agape* demands a relational distance. Without *agape's* further (re)creative act, creation's forsakenness necessarily leads to its realization of isolation, disconnection, and despair, as it is impossible for creation to create correspondences to God on its own. Original creation is trapped in the bind of being called to respond as God's Other, but only being able to respond by "unavoidably" sinning.[25] Creation, in its hopelessness, simultaneously must act and must wait in hope for *agape's* (re)creation.

Summarizing our argument at this point is helpful. First, the difference between *philia* and *agape* allows Moltmann to make a distinction between the relationships of the divine communion and the relationship of God with creation. This distinction is important as *philia* is characteristic of a perichoretic indwelling that does not allow for the free response of the Other. *Agape* allows for a different Other. The space of difference comes to be by a divine withdrawal.[26] However, the space of difference remains within the divine communion. Hence, Moltmann can simultaneously talk about a divine abandonment of creation and creation as an overflow of divine love.[27]

---

25. While Moltmann argues that the *nihil* "only acquires this menacing character" through human sin and godlessness (*GC* 88), it is difficult to see how humans can avoid sinning and thereby realizing the *nihil*, as they must act in a godforsaken space. Self-isolation as the condition of original creation must lead to a realization of annihilating nothingness.

26. See Grenz, *The Social God*, 42ff.

27. Jansen wonders if "Moltmann's distinction between necessary and free love (*philia* and *agape*) is at all helpful in understanding the nature of love . . . it is difficult to understand how such terms would clarify the human experience of love" (*Relationality*, 137).

Second, in understanding creation as divinely forsaken Moltmann can reject the "now and always" view of reality. Neither God nor creation can simply be identified with what "is." Both God and creation must be understood as dynamic and open to the possible. From its inception, original creation is identified as "the world which is passing away" (*COG* 280). Creation awaits its redemption through the overcoming of its condition of being godforsaken. Original creation is countered and surpassed by "the world which is coming to be." As creative, *agape* calls both *creatio ex nihilo* and *nova creatio* into being. The presence of divine love as *agape* implies that even as godforsaken, creation is destined for good. It is never outside of God. Creation flows from and returns to the divine communion of love. In spite of its being originally disconnected from God, creation remains fundamentally "an expression of his love."

Just as creation is understood to spring from the overflow of *philia*, it can also be said that the Father "creates out of the powers and energies of his own Spirit" (*TK* 113). This pouring out of the Spirit is not the same as divinizing creation, or equating creation with God, but these are "relationships of *mutuality* which describe a cosmic community of living between God the Spirit and all his created beings" (*GC* 14).[28] Creation is viewed "as a divine overflowing or 'emanation'" (*TK* 113). From inner-trinitarian life "the Holy Spirit is 'poured out'" (ibid.). In this cosmic community, the Spirit relates to creation by "'indwelling', 'sympathizing', 'participating', 'accompanying', 'enduring', 'delighting', and 'glorifying'" (*GC* 14).

Within the godforsaken space, the Spirit is agapic: "An intricate web of unilateral, reciprocal and many-sided relationships. In this network of relationships, 'making', 'preserving', 'maintaining' and 'perfecting' are certainly the great *one-sided* relationships" (ibid.).[29] The energies of the Spirit are poured into creation as the Spirit "fills everything with its own life" (*TK* 113). The Father breathes life into creation by "breathing forth" the Spirit. As such, "the Spirit is the efficacious power of the Creator and the power that quickens created beings" (*GC* 96).

---

28. See Wood, "From Barth's Trinitarian Christology," for his analysis of the development of the idea of the Spirit in relation to Barth's thought.

29. It is in these one-sided relationships that the Spirit is active in the movement of creation. Dabney argues in "Advent" that the exclusion of God from the world in *TH* results in a lack of any significant pneumatology, as "the Spirit of God is, like the resurrected Son and the Father, shut up in the future and away from the present" (94). Furthermore, Dabney says, "central to that effort to overcome the problem of discontinuity in the tradition [Moltmann] had inherited, was the gradual turn to pneumatology" (ibid., 96). Bauckham makes a similar point: "It was through pneumatology that Moltmann softened the Barthian exclusiveness of the Word" (*The Theology of Jürgen Moltmann*, 45).

The Spirit's presence in forsaken creation must be understood as *agape* inasmuch as "this power is itself creative" (ibid.). The presence of the Father's creative power in creation through the Spirit shows that "the Creator himself is present in his creation" (ibid.). But his presence is not a perichoretic indwelling. The Spirit as manifesting *agape* exists as that which calls non-existent reality into being. By being present in his own creation, "God preserves his creation against the annihilating Nothingness" (ibid.). Preservation is not to be understood as a protection of creation's intrinsic goodness; rather, Moltmann suggests that the surpassing of transient reality does not mean the *nihil* has the final word. The Spirit, which gives life to all of creation, also preserves the space of creation for God's future indwelling by acting "against the hardenings of sin and the petrifaction of death" (*SL* 56). The Spirit safeguards creation by keeping open the possibility of the future. There is a linking between the Spirit's "creating, his preserving, his renewing and his consummating activity" (*GC* 12). The presence of the Spirit in forsaken creation allows creation to be understood as "ontic promise and the ontological parable, the real promise and the real symbol of the coming kingdom of God" (*HTG* 130). The presence of the Spirit points to the eschatological fulfillment of the promise and the Father's new creative activity. Moltmann describes the Spirit as that which "bridge[s] the difference between Creator and creature, the actor and the act, the master and the work—a difference which otherwise seems to be unbridged by any relation at all" (*TK* 113).

Given our understanding of Moltmann's view of creation and the concurrent, contradictory movements in the original act of creation and creation's restoration, we can add the following elements to our previous diagram.

Divine Love 51

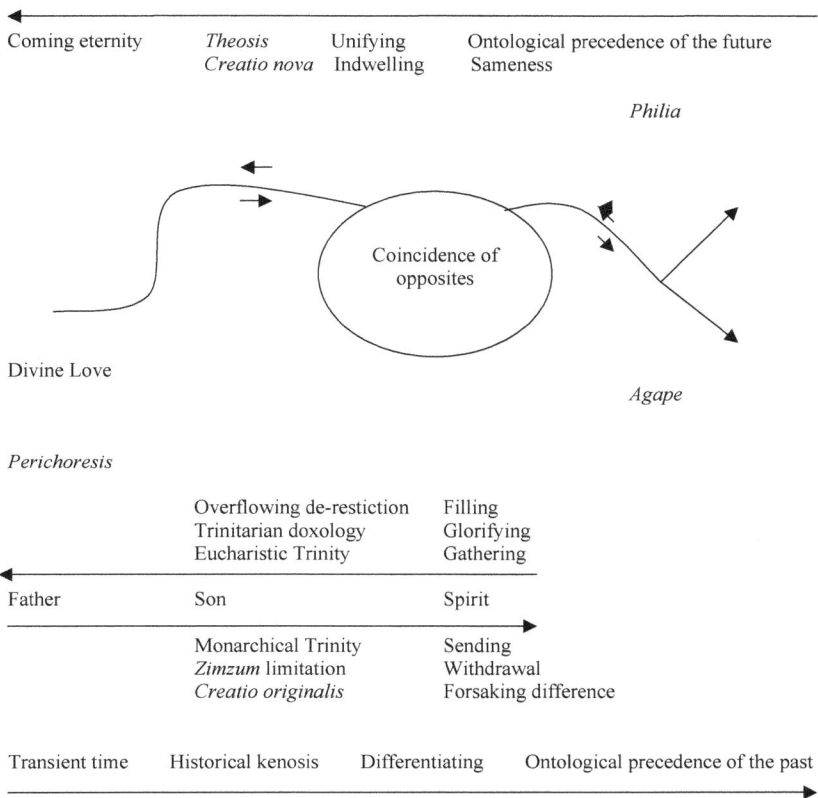

Figure 3

In this chapter I have argued that Moltmann's sustained account of difference/sameness that permeates his entire corpus is readily displayed in his discussion of love. The difference between *agape* (love for the unlike) and *philia* (love for the like) is simultaneously accounted for in terms of opposition and unity. In the next chapter we will examine how Jesus Christ as the nexus of *agape* and *philia* brings the hope of a new creation through his crucifixion and resurrection.

CHAPTER 4

Jesus Christ as Cosmic Turning Point

Identity in Infinite Contradiction

SIMULTANEOUSLY, THE PENETRATING, INDWELLING movement of *philia* promises a future redeemed creation that is coming to be, and the forsaking, creative movement of *agape* produces an original creation that is passing away. Or, to say it another way, the initial creative act prepares the way for the salvific act. For Moltmann, the initial creative act of *agape* and the subsequent (re)creative act of *philia* signify the two opposing, concurrent movements that generate the dynamic nature of reality. Whether this "coincidentia oppositorium" is described as the tension between present and future, forsakenness and hope, or history and promise, each of these contrasting pairs point to the ways in which divine love moves.

In this chapter we will examine how Moltmann understands the incarnation, Good Friday, and Easter as revealing Jesus Christ to be the unity of the contradictory movements of *philia* and *agape*, and God's contradiction of creation's contradiction. Subsequently, the role of the Spirit in the redemptive process will be evaluated in the light of the tension apparent between creation and (re)creation. Once again, so will I argue, we will see the emergence of basic contradictory motifs in Moltmann's thought and their ultimate resolution in an all-surpassing and all-embracing unity of God.

The Incarnation for Creation

The dynamic between creation and (re)creation leads to a distinction among what are called the 'times' of creation:

> So if "creation" is to be the quintessence of the whole divine creative activity, the corresponding doctrine of creation must then embrace creation in the beginning, creation in history, and the

creation of the End-time: *creatio originalis–creatio continua–creatio nova*. "Creation" is the term for God's initial creation, his historical creation, and his perfected creation. The idea of God's unity is preserved only through the concept of creation as a meaningful coherent process. This process acquires its significance from its eschatological goal. (*GC* 55)

The intention for original creation was never to remain godforsaken. Within abandoned creation, *agape* has the potential to bring into existence that which is not and establish connections between inner-trinitarian life and creation. Creaturely existence is within a forsaken space, yet that space remains within God. The hope of creation is for the redemption of the forsaken space and of the abandoned creation by God. In the redemptive movement, the *philia* of the perichoretic community transforms into *agape*. But *agape*, having already established a space of difference, comes to create connections between God and *creatio originalis* by revealing "the perfected self-communication of the triune God" (*TK* 116) within the *nihil*. This perfected self-communication is the second person of the Trinity incarnate. In the incarnation, the Father achieves his desire; that is, he "acquires a twofold counterpart for his love: his Son and his image . . . he experiences . . . the response of the Son, which is self-evident—a matter of course—and the free response of the image" (*TK* 121).[1]

This need of original creation as God's different Other for the "perfected self-communication" of the inner-trinitarian community means "the Son of God did not become man simply because of the sin of men and women, but rather for the sake of perfecting creation. So the Son of God would have become man even if the human race had remained without sin" (*TK* 116). The "intention" of the incarnation preceded any actualization of the *nihil* as the Son's embodiment as the self-communication of God "fulfills this design of creation" (*TK* 117). The result is that "Christology is more than the presupposition for soteriology" (*TK* 115). Because creation arises from the Father's eternal love for the Son "it is from eternity that the Son has been destined to be the Logos, the mediator of creation" (*TK* 112).[2]

1. Goetz argues in "Karl Barth" that *agape* seems to be understood as *eros* in Moltmann's description of the Father's love for the Son. He concludes that "Creation is the inevitable love child of the *eros* of the Father for the Son" (24).

2 Compare with LaCugna's summary of Gregory Palamas' position: "Union with God according to hypostasis occurs only in Christ" (*God for Us*, 184). Note also her insight that "the influence of Pseudo-Dionysius is apparent in Gregory's description" (ibid., 185). In making such connections with Moltmann, a pattern of influence begins to emerge, flowing from Heraclitus and Pseudo-Dionysus. See also Marion, "In the Name," for his interaction with Dionysus.

There is an indissoluble link between the Son and creation from eternity: "the idea of the Son's mediating function in creation (which is necessary for the trinitarian concept) stands in correlation both to the idea of the incarnation of God's Son, and to the idea of the lordship of the Son of Man" (ibid.).[3] From the very beginning, and even though it is grounded in divine love, *creatio originalis*'s relationship with the Father has not been immediate. The Father's withdrawal to allow the space of difference meant that an intermediary had to bridge the gap between the Father and *creatio originalis*. The incarnation is viewed as a necessary transaction linking the opposing movements of *creatio originalis* and *creatio nova*.[4] Isolated from the perichoretic community, *creatio originalis* could only receive divine love by God becoming like the different Other.

The Son is the bond that maintains the identity through the times of creation.[5] *Creatio originalis* is the creation that comes to be in the forsaken space that is in need of fulfillment by the Son. This is the first pulse of *agape*. Creation here moves historically towards its "eschatological goal." *Creatio nova* arrives from the future to overcome/complete original creation. Here the incarnate Son enacts the second pulse of *agape* and God becomes "all in all." *Creatio continua* describes the current situation in which both of these movements are simultaneously experienced. The incarnate Jesus Christ is the linchpin, swivel, flip, or turning point between *creatio originalis* and *creatio nova*, as he both bears the burden of godforsakenness and reveals the way of overcoming such forsakenness.[6]

Incarnation as Mediation

In the incarnation Jesus Christ mediates between the perichoretic community and *creatio originalis*. As shown, mediation was necessary from the moment creation came to be in a god-forsaken space. Creation's rejection of God through its self-reliant activity, thus actualizing the *nihil*, merely changed the form in which the Son was incarnate, not the need for the

---

3. See also *CG* 94ff.

4. As Bauckham explains, "in principle there is no necessary continuity from this life and this world to eternal life" (*God Will Be All in All*, 8).

5. Gresham concludes, "Moltmann's rejection of a Christology from above limits his ability to describe adequately the Christology implied by his trinitarian theology" ("The Social Model" 338). I would suggest this tension is further evidence of the two contrary movements in Moltmann's thought.

6. Cobb identifies a problem with "the way in which Moltmann connects, or almost identifies, the history of salvation events to which the New Testament witnesses with an everlasting tri-unity in God" ("Reply," 174).

incarnate Son. The presence of sin meant that Christ had to take the form of a servant and suffer in his incarnation. In a creation where the *nihil* has been actualized, the incarnate Son "humiliates himself, accepting and adopting threatened and perverted human nature in its entirety, making it part of his eternal life" (*TK* 121).

Here we can begin to make fuller sense of the claim that "the divinity of God is kenosis" (UL 120). In creating, God has withdrawn into himself for the sake of a different Other. The expectation was always present that God must enter into the forsakenness, but now in a sinful creation divine love as *agape* means that the Son must experience the cross. In the movement of *creatio originalis,* the Son must be abandoned in order for God's perfected self-communication to resonate within the community of creation that has never experienced the less distinctive boundaries of *perichoresis*. In the cross, *agape* again becomes creative as divine love "communicates itself by overcoming its opposite" (*TK* 107). God bears the suffering of rejection as "he enters into the situation of their sin and God-forsakenness . . . (and) accepts and adopts it himself, making it part of his eternal life. Through this "outward incarnation" and "inward self-humiliation" God overcomes the opposition (*TK* 119). This act "serves the reconciliation and redemption of men and women," and at the same time "God becomes the God who identifies himself with men and women to the point of death and beyond" (ibid.).[7]

Eschatology and the Ontic Reversal

The cross is the perichoretic community's identification with forsaken reality.[8] However, the cross of Jesus is never to be considered in isolation from the resurrection just as one can never consider *creatio originalis* in isolation from *creatio nova*.[9] Any deliberation on the cross necessarily entails the resurrection and any consideration of the resurrection must include the cross. Each event represents the opposing movements of reality. In historical time; that is, in the movement of the world that is passing away,

---

7. Bauckham points out that for Moltmann, in the incarnation "God is not like us but actually one of us" (*The Theology of Jürgen Moltmann*, 68). However, in a more critical article, Bauckham maintains that "we do not relate to Jesus the incarnate Son in the same way as we relate to God the Father" ("Jürgen Moltmann's *The Trinity*," 161), raising the questions of identity and differentiation that plague Moltmann's thought.

8. See Thévenaz, "Le Dieu crucifié."

9. Wiebe is concerned that Moltmann's "emphasis on eschatology, his concentration on the future, prevents him from giving full weight to the place of God's action in Christ in the present" ("Revolution," 107).

"Jesus first died and was then raised" (*COG* 184).¹⁰ Eschatologically; that is, in the movement of the world coming to be, "he died as the risen Christ and was made flesh as the one who was to come" (ibid.). Thinking eschatologically in relation to the cross results in "the reversal of the noetic and the ontic order" (ibid.).¹¹ Noetically, the experience of the cross has chronological priority and the cross comes to symbolize the movement of history towards original creation's annihilation. Ontically, the experience of the resurrection has a logical priority, and Easter comes to symbolize the new creative act that overcomes creation's forsakenness.

At the same time, along these lines, "the incarnation of the Son is not something transitional. It is and remains to all eternity" (*TK* 119). Indeed, it is not speaking anthropomorphically to say that "if . . . the Son's incarnation is his true humanity, then the incarnation reveals the true humanity of God" (*TK* 118). It belongs to "the quintessence of his divinity itself" (ibid.). Jesus Christ is from all eternity the hinge for both God and creation. In the incarnation of the Son both *creatio originalis* and *creatio nova* are intimately connected. Because of the linking of sameness and difference in Jesus Christ, he can function as the lens or prism through which reality is seen in its totality. The incarnate Son is both the one crucified and the one resurrected. The play between Good Friday and Easter is significant for Moltmann.¹² Good Friday is creation in its utter despair and forsakenness. Easter is creation redeemed by God. As the movements of both *philia* and *agape* exist in each event, the two events can never be separated; they are, so to speak, two sides of the same coin. The resurrected one is always the crucified one, and the crucified one is always the resurrected one. As both the same and the different Other, the incarnate Son Jesus Christ is "wholly and utterly" God's communication of himself. God's desire is to communicate "himself to his like and to his Other. God is love. That means he is responsive love, both in essence and freely" (*TK* 59).

In such a perspective, we can understand the claim that "the disciples' proclamation that he was raised from the dead . . . arises from, and is made necessary by, the comparing of the two contradictory experiences which

---

10. Olson maintains that for Moltmann "historical events become determinative of God's eternal being" ("Trinity and Eschatology," 217).

11. As Torrance notes, for Moltmann "it is particularly through the death of Christ on the cross, and his cry of godforsakenness, that our understanding is opened to the Trinity" (*The Christian Doctrine of God*, 54).

12. Olson explains that for Moltmann "the event of the cross, as central and determinative as it is, is not exclusively determinative of the inner trinitarian life of God, but is dependent upon the kingdom of the Father in creation and the kingdom of the Spirit in the liberation and union of creation in God" ("Trinity and Eschatology," 220).

they have of Christ" (*TH* 198). Experiencing the cross of Christ means for them, on the one hand, "the experience of the god-forsakenness of God's ambassador—that is, an absolute *nihil* embracing also God" (ibid.). Experiencing Christ as the one raised from the dead, on the other hand, "means for them the experience of the nearness of God in the god-forsaken one, of the divineness of God in the crucified and dead Christ—that is, a new totality which annihilates the total *nihil*" (ibid.). Moltmann summarizes that these two experiences "stand in radical contradiction to each other" (ibid.). But it is in this total contradiction that there is a "process of identification" (ibid.). In a nutshell, this harmony in contradiction is the genius of what I am calling Moltmann's contradictory monism.

Identity in Infinite Contradiction

God assumes the contradiction between the godforsaken creation and the kingdom of God. God does not turn away from his opposite, but embraces the crucified Jesus and godforsaken creation in their difference. In the resurrection, the raising of Jesus to life, "God created continuity in this radical discontinuity."[13] The incarnate Son is the lens into this continuity as "the fundamental event in the Easter appearances then manifestly lies in the revelation of the identity and continuity of Jesus in the total contradiction of cross and resurrection, of god-forsakenness and the nearness of God" (*TH* 199). The result of the dialectic of the cross is "an identity in total contradiction" (*TH* 199). *Creatio nova* is both continuous and discontinuous with *creatio originalis*. Jesus' identity is "in, but not above and beyond, cross and resurrection" (*TH* 200).

The meanings of the cross and resurrection cannot be conflated with one another, as both are an inherent part of Jesus' identity.[14] Moltmann insists, "the Alpha and Omega are the same as far as the Person is concerned . . . But they are not the same where the reality of the event is concerned" (*TH* 229). The history of *creatio originalis* climaxes on Good Friday; God counters with a *creatio nova* on Easter. Good Friday and Easter are two sides of the same coin.[15] Death is the absence of life, which is indicative of godforsakenness, but also represents an emptiness that God fills. Reestablishing a relationship between the godforsaken *creatio originalis* and the God who comes from the future is possible because "in all the qualitative difference of cross and resurrection Jesus is the same" (*TH* 85). Even

---

13. Bauckham, *The Theology of Jürgen Moltmann*, 33.
14. See ibid., 32ff.
15. See Pannenberg, *Systematic Theology*, 1:314ff.

in the forsakenness of the cross, Jesus is the risen one. In the nexus of *creatio originalis* and *creatio nova*, "this identity in infinite contradiction is theologically understood as an event of identification, an act of the faithfulness of God" (ibid.). The identity of Jesus in the cross and resurrection is significant because "God reveals himself as 'God' where he shows himself as the same and is thus known as the same" (*TH* 116). In God's identification with Jesus, he becomes "identifiable . . . (as) he identifies himself with himself in the historic act of his faithfulness" (ibid.). The identity of Jesus within the contradiction "is the ground of the hope which carries faith through the trials of the god-forsaken world and of death" (*TH* 85).

For Moltmann, the cross and resurrection are the contradiction-in-unity events par excellence. They manifest both the contradiction of *philia* and *agape* and their simultaneous underlying unity. *Philia* first transforms, or "flips," into *agape* in order to allow for the difference necessary for the creation of God's different Other. *Agape's* second "flip" leads to *creatio nova*. Through embodying the forsakenness of *agape*, Jesus becomes the perfected self-communication of God to an abandoned creation. In this movement identity "exists only through the contradiction" (*TH* 200). Identity is dependent upon two opposing, concurrent movements in an "open dialectic, which will find its resolving synthesis only in the eschaton of all things" (*TH* 201).

Identity exists in the opposing movements of reality. Even though in the cross we see the *creatio originalis* that is passing away and in the resurrection we see the *creatio nova* of the world that is coming to be, the eschatological resolution is not yet complete. From the perspective of history, the *creatio nova* has not fully arrived nor has *creatio originalis* been entirely overcome. After the Christ event, oppositional pairs characterize the age: the past and the future, the cross and the resurrection, history and promise. This in-between stage is *creatio continua*. Tension is located in post resurrection creation, as experienced historically, because the dialectical process continues. Knowledge of the future of creation and of Christ remains provisional as "the future of Christ . . . can be stated only in promises" (*TH* 202). The coming eschaton of Christ in which the *creatio nova* will be fully realized has not yielded noetic certainty in the *creatio continua*, hence "promise stands between knowing and not knowing, between necessity and possibility, between that which is not yet and that which already is" (*TH* 203).

Historically, creation is still experiencing the reality of the *nihil* in its godforsakenness and must live in anticipation of its redemption and the return of its Messiah. While in reality's eschatological direction God has arrived in the resurrection of Jesus, God's arrival is yet to be fully experienced historically. Even though God's presence in creation has been manifested and promised in God's identification with the crucified Christ by raising him to life, *creatio originalis* and *creatio nova*'s movements have yet to be fully reconciled. Living in the time of promise means awaiting the final identity of Christ as "all the titles of Christ point messianically forward" (ibid.). The dialectic of cross and resurrection continues as god-forsaken creation awaits its redemption and as God moves from the future towards creation.

In the *creatio continua* "the resurrection and the future of God must manifest themselves not only in the case of the god-forsakenness of the crucified Jesus Christ, but also in that of the god-forsakenness of the world" (*TH* 169). The cosmic process is affected by the cross and resurrection of Jesus as "the whole world is now involved in God's eschatological process of history, not only the world of men and nations" (*TH* 137). The identity of Jesus through Good Friday and Easter results not in "a mere return to life as such, but as a conquest of the deadliness of death—as a conquest of god-forsakenness . . ." (*TH* 211).[16]

Creation and the Internal Suffering of the Trinity

The redemption of creation from its forsaken history depends, for Moltmann, upon God's ability to suffer the forsakenness of *creatio originalis*. In identifying with creation through the incarnate Son, God takes the suffering of his different Other upon himself. God's love that bears the pain of creation is not only an external relationship; rather, "it also affects the trinitarian fellowship in God himself" (*TK* 24). We can investigate the depth of this suffering by once again looking at *agape* and *philia*. *Agape* as like for the unlike is also a suffering love. As we already have examined, the movement of divine love between God and creation in the direction of *creatio originalis* is a transmutation of *philia* into *agape*. *Agape* abandons as it calls into being that which did not exist—God's different Other. But *agape* is also the divine love found within forsaken creation. The love of the incarnate Son for *creatio originalis* has to be *agape*. Only the love that suffers and calls into being that which does not exist can characterize the cross and resurrection. But now the divine suffering is described as affecting "the Trinitarian fellowship in God himself." In this movement, *agape*

---

16. Peters summarizes Moltmann's answer to this question: "it is the God who is love and who suffers because of this love who is revealed to us in scripture" (*God as Trinity*, 112).

transmutes, or "flips," back into *philia* and carries suffering into the perichoretic community.

In *agape* becoming *philia*, "the extra-trinitarian suffering and the inner-trinitarian suffering correspond" (*TK* 25); a "divine passion which God suffers for us" and a "divine passion between the Father and the Son in the Trinity" (ibid.). The suffering that God endures and embraces through the cross of his Son is not merely the pain Jesus bore in his humanity. Moltmann is not satisfied to speak only of the godforsakenness of the Son on the cross. On the cross, while the Son suffers from being forsaken, "the Father also suffers the forsakenness of the Son."[17] Though initially the suffering of the forsakenness by the Son and the pain of the abandoning of the Son by the Father do not correspond, ultimately "the Passion of Christ also affects God himself and becomes the Passion of God."[18]

The initial lack of correspondence between the suffering of the Son and the suffering of the Father manifests the difference between the Son's *agape* and the Father's *philia* within the divine community.[19] In the dynamics of the Father's forsaking of the Son, the Son's being forsaken, the suffering of the Father in his love for the forsaken one in his death, and the suffering of the Son in his love as he is forsaken by the Father, Moltmann argues that the pain itself is taken up into the Father's life and thereby into the triune community. In taking the suffering into the divine community, the suffering of God becomes an intrinsic and necessary part of triune relations. The connection is so deep "we can only talk about God's suffering in trinitarian terms" (ibid.). The suffering of divine love takes place not only in "the redeeming acts of God outwards" (*TK* 24), but also within the divine life.[20]

Once pain and suffering become a necessary part of inner-trinitarian life, they are shared in the giving and receiving of *philia* in *perichoresis*. This (re)definition of *philia* in terms of a shared suffering produces a "retroactive effect" (*TK* 161) on divine life. Eschatology supercedes history as "the pain of the cross determines the inner life of the triune God from eternity to eternity" (ibid.).[21] Divine suffering is not a suffering from cre-

17. *The Passion for Life*, 23.

18. Ibid.

19. Thompson notes that in Moltmann there is "a trinitarian theology that combines the cross and divine suffering" (*Modern Trinitarian Perspectives*, 61). Suffering is not merely present in Jesus Christ's human nature, but at the heart of divine life.

20. But as Jansen points out, "the question still remains as to whether the Father loves what is like in the suffering Son . . . or the unlike?" (*Relationality*, 137).

21. Ahlers asks the question: "In short, it appears essential to state that God was present on the cross. But is it legitimate to invert this statement and say that the cross is also present

ation. Suffering does not move from the external creation into divine life. Rather, "the divine suffering of love outwards is grounded in the pain of love within" (*TK* 25). Creation's fallenness neither initiates nor determines the divine suffering for Moltmann. Rather, divine suffering precedes and makes possible creation. In the overcoming of *creatio originalis* by *creatio nova,* divine life changes from what is into what will be, "even though the divine relationship to the world is primarily determined by that inner relationship. The growth of knowledge of the immanent Trinity from the saving experience of the cross of Christ makes this necessary."[22] In and through *agape* becoming *philia,* the suffering of God for the world—"extra-trinitarian suffering"—and the divine passion between Father, Son, Spirit, and creation correspond.

The Suffering Spirit

Working with the assertion that suffering is found within the perichoretic community, it is not unexpected to find the Spirit also involved in God's identification with forsaken creation.[23] Divine suffering does not initiate, rather it precedes and makes possible creation. Both the Father and the Son identified with creation through their sharing of creation's suffering. For the Spirit to identify with creation and allow it to participate in divine life there must also be a sharing of creation's suffering.[24] Moltmann interprets the description of the Spirit as "descending" upon Christ as pointing to the "self-restriction and self-humiliation of the eternal Spirit" (*SL* 61). Moltmann argues that the Spirit both leads and accompanies Jesus.[25] In accompanying Jesus, the Spirit is "drawn into [Jesus'] sufferings, and becomes his companion in suffering" (*SL* 62). As Jesus' companion in suffering, "the

---

in God?" ("Theory of God," 250). While Moltmann would agree that a distinction must be kept between the two statements, he would also affirm that God's presence at the cross means the cross is part of divine life.

22. For an interesting article comparing Kazo Kitamora's view of divine suffering with Moltmann's, see Kuratmatsu, "Die gegenwörtige Kreuzestheologie."

23. Much recent work has been done on Moltmann's understanding of the Holy Spirit. For example, see Yoo, *The Spirit of Liberation*, and Althouse, *Spirit of the Last Days.*

24. LaCugna argues that, "if the Holy Spirit is seen primarily as the intradivine bond of love between Father and Son (*filioque*), then the Spirit's sanctifying power is seen as extrinsic to the creature" (*God for Us,* 297).

25. Waite, in his analysis of Moltmann, asks: "But if the suffering of God is manifest in the separation of the Father and the Son, in the abandonment of the Son by the Father, how are these persons united so that they may constitute God?" (*Theism, Atheism,* 98). He then answers, "it is the Holy Spirit that unites the Father and the Son in their separation" (ibid.).

Spirit is the transcendent side of Jesus' immanent way of suffering" (ibid.). Like the Father and the Son, the Spirit's suffering involves a self-restriction and self-humiliation. Hence, "the 'condescendence' of the Spirit leads to the progressive kenosis of the Spirit, together with Jesus" (ibid.).

Here again clearly the Spirit's connection with *creatio originalis* is *agape*. But the kenosis of the Spirit, unlike that of the Father and Son, is not an end unto itself. The kenosis of the Spirit allows for the identification and involvement of the Spirit in the Son's suffering and "it is precisely his suffering with the Son to the point of death on the cross which makes the rebirth of Christ from the Spirit inwardly possible" (*SL* 68). The Spirit is key in the countering movement of *creatio nova*, as through *agape*'s creative powers the Spirit "participates in the dying of the Son in order to give him new 'life from the dead'" (ibid.). Once again the reversal from the movement of *agape* as forsaking to the movement of *agape* as resurrecting is precipitated by the incarnation of the Son in an abandoned creation. In spite of the emphasis placed on the incarnation of the Son, Good Friday and Easter must be understood as thoroughly trinitarian, as "[the Spirit] accompanies Christ to his end, he can make this end the new beginning" (ibid.).

Agape and its *creatio originalis* are kenotic. The cross represents the culmination of the emptying of the Father, Son, and Spirit for creation. This kenotic movement in which God empties himself is transformed in the Christ event as the presence of God overcomes the emptiness in *agape*'s *creatio nova*. Indwelt by the Spirit of life, creation arises from the dead.

Agape towards *Theosis*

Creatio nova is not the result of a divine withdrawal; instead, "in the gift and through the powers of the Holy Spirit a new divine presence is experienced in creation" (*GC* 96). Through the presence of the Spirit, "God the creator takes up his dwelling in his creation and makes it his home" (ibid.). The eschatological movement is towards a re-filling of the godforsaken space. Creation arrives at its completion "in the operation and indwelling of the Spirit, the creation of the Father through the Son, and the reconciliation of the world with God through Christ, arrive at their goal" (ibid.). Or, phrased differently, "the presence and the efficacy of the Spirit is the eschatological goal of creation and reconciliation" (ibid.). The Spirit is understood to be "the One who gives life to the world and allows it to participate in God's eternal life" (*GC* 97).

The perichoretic community identifies with forsaken creation through a kenosis that leads to divine presence.[26] Divine *agape*'s creativity in the midst of forsakenness reclaims creation as its own. Finally, a community between God and his different Other emerges. But the role of the different Other has been altered for the sake of the community. In *creatio originalis* "creation exists because the eternal love communicates himself creatively to his Other," whereas *creatio nova* "exists because the eternal love seeks fellowship and desires response in freedom" (*TK* 59). Likewise, having a different Other freely acting was not the hope of creating a different Other. Creating a free Other is not enough, because "self-communicating love . . . only becomes fulfilled when its love is returned" (*TK* 117). God is not fulfilled in the freedom of the Other, but in the free acceptance by the Other of God's gift of fellowship through mutual indwelling. In the desired perichoretic community of inner-trinitarian and extra-trinitarian relations, God "only came fully to himself by virtue of that Other's response to his love" (*TK* 107).

The Deification of Creation

Freedom of the different Other is transcended when God returns creation to himself as the very conditions of freedom are overcome in the warm confines of *perichoresis*. God's ultimate creative desire is not that a different Other exists, but that the different Other is in community with him. God's intent never was for creation to remain disconnected from him in a forsaken space, but that through the opposition a greater unity would form as God (re)filled the space of creation.[27] The promise at the initial separation of God and his different Other was that God would delimit the space within himself and fully indwell the Other as the Other had dwelt within him.

The Father's desire for community with his Other affirms the Other's difference while simultaneously overriding difference for the sake of community. His giving love is fulfilled when he "finds bliss in the eternal response to his love through the Son . . . he also desires to find bliss through this other's responsive love" (*TK* 117). Because God "needs" the response of his different Other in order to find his bliss, which is to experience

---

26. Peters insightfully points out that Moltmann echoes Hegel when "he says the Trinity achieves its integrative unity principally by uniting itself with the history of the world" (*God as Trinity*, 110).

27. Moltmann's appeal to the notion of deification has a long theological tradition rooted in the Cappadocians; particularly in Basil, Gregory of Nazianzus, and Gregory of Nyssa.

intimate community with all of reality, opposition must be overcome. The overcoming of opposition is not merely a removal of sin's actualization of the *nihil*, but an annihilation of the very conditions of *creatio originalis*. Moltmann summarizes, "if the misery of creation lies in sin as separation from God, then salvation consists in the gracious acceptance of the creature into communion with God. Salvation lies in this union. The union with God of what is separated is not just an external union" (*HTG* 87). The divine unity achieved in the perichoretic relationships of the Trinity overflows into creation through God's excessive giving to/for the Other. The *agape* that was a withdrawal becomes an *agape* that fills, as "the unity of the Father, the Son, and the Spirit is then the eschatological question about the consummation of the trinitarian history of God. The unity of the three Persons of this history must consequently be understood as a communicable unity and as an open, inviting unity, capable of integration" (*TK* 149).

Through a kenosis that fills, the divine community draws creation closer and closer together. Creation then is internally joined with the divine community. This union is not the connection of God with creation, but the transformation of identity, as God's different Other becomes part of the divine community through an "eschatological becoming-one-with God" (*GC* 229).[28] The process of human beings becoming one with God is *theosis* (ibid.).[29] That is, wherever God has emptied himself, he eventually returns to fill that space with his presence.[30] This (re)filling simultaneously in/validates the movement of kenosis. It validates the kenosis by

---

28. Gregory Palamas distinguishes between divine essence (*ousia*) and divine energies (*energeiai*). While God's essence is unknowable and imparticible, the energies which are modalities of God's action in the world are knowable and open to participation. For a full treatment, see Meyendorff, *A Study of Gregory Palamas*. For a more concise consideration, see Lacugna, *God for Us*, chap.6. See also Williams, "The Philosophical Structures of Palamism," wherein he critiques the placing of essence above energies, as "once *ousia* has been 'concretized' into a core of essential life, it will inevitably take on some associations of superiority or ontological priority" (34).

29. Moltmann's use of theosis is always in conjunction with his idea of *perichoresis*. Creation's participation in the Trinity "make's it possible to preserve both the unity and difference of what is diverse in kind" (*COG*, 278). Similarly, Fiddes notes theosis as, "not becoming God, but being incorporated into the fellowship of the divine life" (*Participating in God*, 76). The question of the conditions of that participation has not yet been addressed.

30. Schuurman argues, "hopes for any sort of continuity between creation and re-creation are effectively smashed by predictions that whatever created beings there will be . . . will be divested of temporality, relationality, the possibility for change—stripped of all the limitations the Creator so tenderly set about us and called 'very good'" ("Creation, Eschaton, and Ethics," 50).

recognizing the necessity of opposition for the greater unity. This, after all, is the only way divine love exhausts its desire and achieves its end. But *theosis* also invalidates the difference found in the oppositional space as the new community violates the boundaries previously established for difference. The divine love that was for the different Other is overcome as God replicates himself in his overwhelming giving. Perichoretic love is *philia*, not *agape*.

Divine *agape* for the different Other leads the Other back into the divine community. For true community between God and creation, creation must be "indwelt," "interpenetrated," and "raised up" into divine life.[31] The *agape* found in the *creatio original* relationship between God and his different Other is ultimately transformed into the *philia* of inner-trinitarian relationships. *Creatio nova* is a "friend of God."[32] Despite the painstaking differentiation between *agape* and *philia*, in the end they are the same, for "the love with which God creatively and sufferingly loves the world is no different from the love he himself is in eternity" (*TK* 59).

But the love that God is in eternity lacks difference. Even in the differentiation of the Trinity, sameness dominates the divine community as Father, Son, and Spirit are of one essence. For creation as different Other to become part of the divine community, it must become like God. Moltmann describes the result of God's love for creation: "God's love for his Other is then in actual fact nothing else than the extended love of God for the one like himself. The deification of the world and humanity is the necessary conclusion . . ." (*TK* 107). In *theosis*, creation becomes deified. The divinization of creation results in a perichoretic relationship between God and creation: "God in the world and the world in God" (*GC* 17), in which there is "reciprocal indwelling and mutual interpenetration" (ibid.).[33] This indwelling and interpretation transforms the Other, as "any-

---

31. Cunningham has an excellent discussion regarding problems surrounding the use of "interpenetration" in *These Three Are One*, chap. 5.

32. Zizioulas, in *Being as Communion*, explains that deification leads to a transformation of the biological as it "endow(s) the (biological) with being, to give it true ontology, that is eternal life" (63). Like Moltmann, Zizioulas wants to emphasize both a radical change in creation through theosis and the continuity of creation. Compare with Moltmann's assertion that "through [creation's] participation in God's eschatological presence, 'a world without end' comes into being" (*GC* 184). Hence, LaCugna's point that for Zizioulas the struggle to live as Jesus Christ lived "is not a flight from nature, from body, from eros, from world, but the hypostatization of the biological in a nonbiological way" (*God for Us*, 264) could also describe Moltmann's ethics of discipleship.

33. There is an interesting contrast between Moltmann's synonymous usage of *perichoresis*, interpenetration, and participation with Radical Orthodoxy's use of participation,

one who knows that he is eternally loved by God becomes God's eternal Son. So God is as dependent on him as he is on God" (*TK* 107).

Same, Yet Different

Creation's joining of the divine community means evolving from mediated connection to unmediated fellowship and changing from different Other to same Other. Each of these indicates a change for a created being. But Moltmann counters his assertion that creation is deified with claims asserting creation's difference: "What is Other in confrontation with God is not identical with the otherness of God" (ibid.). In clarifying the statement that God's love makes creation God's son, the argument is made that divine love "does not turn the world into the Son, or make the Son the world" (ibid.). Rather, those who return God's love become 'sons of God' but not "the only begotten Son" (ibid.), as "the distinction between the world process and the inner-trinitarian process must be maintained and emphasized" (ibid.). Difference is promoted as "even in the kingdom of glory the world remains God's creation and will not become God himself" (*GC* 184).

Deification does not mean that "human beings are transformed into gods," but that they "partake of the characteristics and rights of the divine nature through their community with Christ" (*CG* 272). Here Moltmann attempts to protect the eschatological difference in similarity between Creator and creation. Again, as I have represented in the diagram below, the simultaneous assertion of contradictory statements is evident. There is the argument that God and creation remain distinct and the concurrent argument that God's presence overwhelms new creation in the process of deification. While holding the Creator and creation in distinction, there is also the understanding that, in the eschatological refilling of creation with God's presence, God overcomes every self-limitation he previously set, and in the end, Creator and creation are the same.

---

which is claimed as a central theological framework in Milbank, Ward, and Pickstock. For Milbank, participation is understood in a Platonic way "because any alternative configuration perforce reserves a territory independent of God" (*Radical Orthodoxy*, 3). Moltmann would suspect that such a conception is too static.

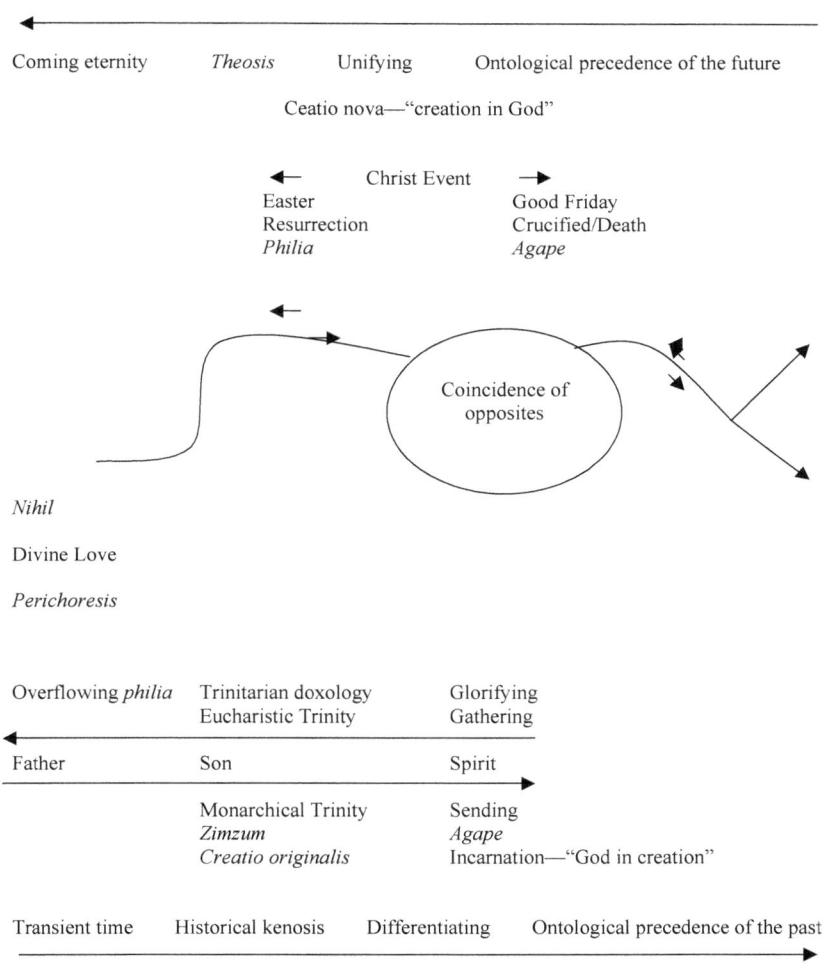

Figure 4

Moltmann highlights the tension in this contradictory state of affairs when he explains that "without the difference between Creator and creature, creation cannot be conceived of at all; but this difference is embraced and comprehended by the greater truth which is what the creation narrative really comes down to, because it is the truth from which it springs: the truth that God is all in all" (*GC* 89). This statement is consistent with Moltmann's privileging of unity, even as the difference continues. Differentiation is not the "greater truth" of Moltmann's thought. Rather, God's goal for the different Other is achieved through his delimitation, whereby the relationship between God and creation becomes a direct fellowship of same Others. The greater truth points to the unity of *perichoresis*, not the differentiation found in kenosis. Kenosis is not the end, but the path to the goal of God's overwhelming presence. *Theosis* needs kenosis as God comes to himself through creation.

CHAPTER 5

The Sabbath Feast of Redemption

Cosmic Perichoresis

As we have seen at the conclusion of chapter 4, Moltmann argues that the unmediated correspondences and connections between created time and inner-trinitarian life result in greater ontological dissimilarity and eschatological similarity. It is striking because he also asserts, as we have also seen, that in redemption the relational space of creation outside of God collapses and "attains to its place in God" (*COG* 307). In God creation finds its "community" through the "reciprocal indwelling" and "mutual interpenetrations" (*GC* 16) of the Father, Son, and Spirit as "in the triune God is the mutuality and the reciprocity of love" (*CG* 17).

In this chapter we will be seeking to understand, as precisely as possible, how Moltmann can simultaneously assert that God penetrates his creation thereby becoming "all in all" even as a greater eschatological dissimilarity between Creator and creation is realized.[1] In pursuing our answer to this question, we will be examining Moltmann's conceptualization of the kingdom of glory, which he also calls the Sabbath feast of redemption. Within this discussion, the relationship between *philia* and *agape* will again ask for our attention. Finally, under the impact of Moltmann's key references to contradiction and unity at crucial junctures of his theology, we will suggest that the fundamental structural features of his thought can be appropriately, and beneficially, understood as a contradictory/harmonic monism.

---

1. Metz, in "Suffering unto God," raises the question of difference when he is critical of the apparent lack of space between God and creation in Moltmann. He sees no room for difference in Moltmann's version of eschatological unity.

Primordial Self-Restriction and Eschatological De-restriction

For Moltmann, we have already established that *creatio originalis* came into existence as unfulfilled.[2] *Creatio originalis* is deficient as God's complete indwelling is incomplete due to God's "primordial self-restrictions" (*COG* 282). From its inception creation awaits its realization through a divine filling.[3] Such completion entails the overcoming of the actualized *nihil* by God's kenosis and by creation's fulfillment by God's *theosis* into the forsakenness of *agape*'s originating withdrawal.[4]

While God may not fully dwell in *creatio originalis*, God's "immanence in creation" is still experienced under these conditions (*GC* 280). The simultaneity of creation's lack and God's movement of redemption towards creation are manifest in what Moltmann calls "the Sabbath of creation." God has not yet come to complete rest in creation, but neither is he absent. The Sabbath represents both the promised presence of "the completion of creation" and "the revelation of God's reposing existence in his creation" (*GC* 288). This reposing existence is "not a created grace" (*GC* 281), characterizing the work of the cross; rather, the Sabbath "is the uncreated grace of God's presence for the whole of creation" (ibid.).

This presence, for Moltmann, is meant to be experienced in the forsakenness, as is evident in the giving of the Sabbath commandment to Israel. The Sabbath commandment is the way to be followed as it prepares creation for "its true future" (*GC* 276) and thereby anticipates the completion of creation. As revelation, the Sabbath "manifests the world's identity as creation, sanctifies it, and blesses it" (ibid.). In the midst of forsakenness, the Sabbath presence "preserves created things from obliteration" (*GC* 282) until God "comes to himself again" (*GC* 279). This "true future" will be consummated when creation "participate[s] in God's manifested, eternal presence" (*GC* 277) and enjoys God's "eternal Sabbath" (*GC* 288).

---

2. Wood claims that "no one writing in the area of theology has developed more clearly the nature of God as Creator *ex nihilo*" ("From Barth's Trinitarian Christology," 64), but as we have noted, this only identifies one of the movements in Moltmann's thought. The idea of lack in creation has a long history. In the neoplatonic tradition the very idea of love is rooted in this lack.

3. There has been much discussion in the recent years regarding the relationship between creation and eschaton and the issues of continuity and discontinuity. For example, see Schuurman, "Creation, Eschaton, and Ethics," and Volf, "Eschaton, Creation, and Social Ethics."

4. See Pannenberg, *Systematic Theology*, 1:384ff., for his discussion of the proper action of God being his breaking into the world.

The differences noted in Moltmann's pairing of created grace and uncreated grace, Sabbath as revelation and Sabbath as the completion of creation, again point to the structure of his cosmogony. The contradictory movements are increasingly noticeable as Moltmann works out his description of the Sabbath as "the identifying mark of the biblical doctrine of creation" (*GC* 276). In Moltmann's words, creation was "for the sake of the Sabbath" (*GC* 277).[5] Concurrently, "the Sabbath represents creation's redemption" (ibid.). Looking at both movements we can make sense of Moltmann's claim that creation has been brought into being "for the sake of that redemption" (ibid.). God's "creation of a world different from himself is the first step towards realizing . . . the essence of his nature" (*GC* 80). Without creation's original lack, creation's "meaning and destination" (*GC* 278) could not have been in its redemption. Without the Sabbath "feast of creation," creation would have remained incomplete and unfulfilled.

The unity and harmony of these movements is evident when Moltmann explains that "the sabbath of God's creation already contains in itself the redemptive mystery of God's indwelling in his creation" and that "the Sabbath of creation is already the beginning of the kingdom of glory" (*GC* 280). The Sabbath's fulfillment is in the "feast of completion" (*GC* 277), when creation comes to rest in God and "becomes entirely God's creation" (ibid.). Here all of creation experiences the "direct, unmediated presence of God" and "find [its] dwelling" (*GC* 282). The "feast of completion" is the end of time as creation "exit[s] from time into eternity" (*COG* 294). The end of time is "the converse of time's beginning" (ibid.). In contrast to time beginning with God's "primordial self-restrictions," the eschatological moment of the feast of completion involves God's "resolve to redeem" and the "'derestriction' of God" (ibid.). The results of this eschatological delimitation of God are the appearance of "his unveiled glory" (ibid.) in creation and the calling into being of "a kind of cosmic *perichoresis* of divine and cosmic attributes" (*COG* 295).

When God delimits himself in the "feast of completion" creation becomes "partakers of the divine nature" (*COG* 272); all things participate in "the characteristics and rights of the divine nature through their community with Christ, the God-human being" (ibid.). In this feast of redemption, we see "beyond the Sabbath to a future in which God's creation and his revelation will be one" (*COG* 288). Here "we understand redemption as both 'the eternal sabbath' and 'the new creation'" (ibid.).

---

5. See Walsh, "Theology of Hope," 60ff.

Creatio Originalis for the Sake of Creatio Nova

Redemption, for Moltmann, seems to be merely part of the outworking of a genetic cosmogony. Or, it may be more properly understood that creation is simultaneously valued and devalued as it exists "for the sake of redemption."[6] The intent for *creatio originalis* was to be overcome by *creatio nova*. The initial differentiation between God and creation is for the purpose of a greater identity. Both God's and creation's identity are realized eschatologically. Moltmann's doctrine of the incarnation shows redemption to be a predictable stage in the cosmic process. The gift of the Son is not a gracious response to the Fall.[7] Recall the statements that "it is from eternity that the Son has been destined to be the Logos, the mediator of creation" (*TK* 112), and that "the Son of God did not become man simply because of the sin of men and women, but rather for the sake of perfecting creation. So the Son of God would have become man even if the human race had remained without sin" (*TK* 116).

Hence creation's redemption comes with a price. The space of difference is filled with God's presence in the coming eschaton. The incarnation is not a validation of the goodness of creation lost through sin. Rather, it is the revelation that creation is other than God. But for Moltmann, other-than-God means disconnected from God. Creation is God's opposite. If God is life, love, and community, then creation is death, despair, and isolation. The redemption of God's opposite comes through a return. The return of forsaken creation to God and God's return to forsaken creation is the overcoming of God's opposite.

Creatio originalis was formed in the space abandoned by God. God's desire for a different Other was articulated in terms of a spatial struggle. There was an inverse relationship between God and *creatio originalis*. Without God's withdrawal, there was no room for creation. For creation to be, it must be surrounded by the threatening *nihil* and not God's presence. Even if the *nihil* is not actualized until creation acts, there is essentially identification between creation and fall. So it makes perfect sense that the Son must come as incarnate whether or not creation "sins." The isolation and disconnection of God from creation—what I would want to call evil—has taken place prior to the possibility of sin.[8]

---

6. Ibid., 61.

7. Volf, following Moltmann, argues for a primacy of the eschaton, but notes that "primacy is not monopoly" ("Eschaton, Creation, and Social Ethics," 137).

8. See Ansell, "The Call of Wisdom," 31–58, for his discussion of the origin of evil. His re-reading of Genesis 1–3 argues that evil has a human origin, as opposed to Moltmann's theodicy that suggests a divine source.

Moltmann's Economy of Lack/Fulfillment

While Moltmann calls the original task of incarnation the completion of creation, such completion is necessary because of a lack, the lack of God's presence.[9] The complication in talking about a lack in creation is that Moltmann always also speaks of a divine presence. As we have seen, even when creation is understood as an overflow or excess of divine *philia*, the creation of a different Other demands a transformation of *philia* into *agape* and a conceding of space, as "if God were omnipresent in the absolute sense . . . there would be no earthly creation" (*COG* 306). In the yielding of space there is "remoteness from God" and a "spatial distance" which must be understood as a "grace of creation" (ibid.). Remoteness and distance are gracious because they are the conditions for "the liberty of created beings" (ibid.).

In the direction of history there is a presence, but it is the presence of creation *within* God. The divine presence *in* creation is in the eschatological direction; here the incarnate Son has "contradicted creation's contradiction" and the Spirit has been poured out and is indwelling creation. In God's indwelling and fulfillment of creation "the distanced contraposition of the creator *towards* his creation becomes the inner presence of God *in* his creation" (*COG* 307). As creation becomes the "house of God," the relationships between Creator and created beings are "without mediation" (ibid.) and lead to direct participation in the divine life. There is a "mutual indwelling of the world in God and God in the world" (ibid.).

The eschatological, redemptive direction is a necessary counterpart that in/validates the forsaking of *creatio originalis*. The lack of God's presence in the historical movement of creation prepares for the Maker's necessary redemption or fulfilling. Creation's initial lack requires the *agape* of redemption to avoid merely being forsaken and transient, and for completion *agape* must transform into *philia*.

Moltmann stresses we must take seriously "the difference between grace and glory, between reconciliation and redemption" (*HTG* 130). If this difference is not taken seriously "we make too many demands on the covenant and the history of God with men and women, because it is already meant to give what only *theosis*, the visible indwelling of God in his new creation, can give to all creatures" (ibid.). Exactly what does *theosis* give? In order for God to visibly dwell in new creation something must be

---

9. As Schuurman points out, "The 'negative' that is here 'negated' is sin, not creation, but Moltmann does not carefully separate creation and sin" ("Creation, Eschaton, and Ethics," 49). In a similar insight, Walsh concludes that for Moltmann "sin is seen as ontologically constitutive of transitory 'burdened' creatureliness . . ." ("Theology of Hope," 63).

fundamentally new about creation. Yet, forsakenness is the path creation had to take to get to new creation. Forsakenness and disconnection were the conditions of creation coming to be the different Other. At the same time Moltmann insists that God will dwell fully in creation.[10]

Ontological Dissimilarity and Essential Difference

In eschatological mutuality, Moltmann denies the conflation of God and creation: "It is neither necessary for the world to dissolve into God . . . nor for God to be dissolved in the world" (*COG* 307).[11] He emphasizes that distinctions remain in redemption. Boundaries are recognized as "even in the kingdom of glory the world remains God's creation and will not become God himself" (*GC* 184) and "they remain unmingled and undivided" (*COG* 307). As we have previously seen, in the eschaton creation is not "dissolve[d] into God" (ibid.). In affirming dissimilarity, Moltmann does not mean the difference of *creatio originalis*. Rather, as redemption results in the "greater truth" that God is all in all" (*GC* 89), we see Moltmann being consistent here in advocating a position of unity-in-dissimilarity.[12] In his description of divine life, the complete rejection of either unity or dissimilarity would fall short of a thorough description of reality, even a consummated reality. The ability to hold opposing pairs of concepts in tension as a means of describing reality is the genius of contradictory/harmonic monism.

The kenosis of creation is in/validated by the consummating *theosis* that results in an expanded *perichoresis* where "all created things will participate directly and without any mediation in his eternal life" (*GC* 64). The most consistent way to understand what is meant by 'dissimilarity,' as found in the *perichoresis* involving the Trinity and creation, is to compare it with what is found in the distinction between Father, Son, and Spirit. Here we find a much softer boundary for the sake of interpenetration. The capability of both penetrating and being penetrated is necessary for

---

10. Here the full force of Metz's criticism in "Suffering Unto God" regarding the lack of space between God and creation can be appreciated. He focuses on the identification movement in Moltmann in which God delimits himself and refills the once forsaken space. The final oneness is consummated. But in God's self-delimitation, the space necessary for a different Other to exist is overwhelmed with divine presence.

11. Wood suggests that if any theologian has protected "divine otherness from the created order, it is Moltmann!" ("From Barth's Trinitarian Christology," 65).

12. As Pannenberg points out, for Moltmann, "when all things are in God and God is 'all in all,' then the economic Trinity is subsumed in the immanent Trintiy" (*Systematic Theology*, 1:330).

perichoresis's relational unity to exist. While *creatio nova* is not conflated into God, it is fused with the perichoretic community. As penetrated with God's presence, *creatio nova* responds in the safe self-giving and self-receiving atmosphere of *philia*. The softer boundary of creation that participates in the perichoretic community suggests there is no longer a difference of essence between God and *creatio nova*. Essential difference implied opposition, contradiction, and alienation for Moltmann. The dissimilarity of *creatio nova* is within the similarity of the shared mutual indwelling, which means it is not characterized by spatial distance or forsakenness. Creation and the perichoretic God in community are both ontologically dissimilar and eschatologically similar. In Jesus Christ whose identity links both Good Friday and Easter, the community consists simultaneously of a different Other and a same Other.

When humanity encounters God through the cross of Christ, Moltmann argues, the result is being involved in "a realistic divinization" (*CG* 277). In his discussion of the Sabbath Moltmann points out that "the Sabbath is the day when God is present" (*GC* 280). When God is present, creation is completed and both God and creation find rest and peace. The opposition in the forsaken, different Other has ceased, and "in the eschatological kingdom of glory . . . people will finally, wholly and completely be gathered into the eternal life of the triune God—as the early church put it—be 'deified'" (*TK* 213). Instead of being alien to both herself and God, humanity will become a friend of God.

In this panentheism, divine presence and divine absence are defined by the preposition "in." Creation is *in* God or God is *in* creation. *Perichoresis* describes relationships by giving priority to interpenetration. The highest level of relationality is achieved when boundaries are softened and there can be a mutual *in*dwelling. *Creatio originalis* is in God. In this sense, 'in' means that God contains creation. Difference is permitted as the harder boundaries of *agape* keep creation oppositionally distinct in God. God is in *creatio nova*. Creation here is not a container. Rather the softer boundaries of *philia* allow for reciprocity where creation is also in God. In the movement of reciprocity the 'in' points to the identification between the partners. Unity overcomes opposition as difference is transformed by the fusing power of *philia*.

When Moltmann initially establishes the difference between *philia* and *agape* he does so by distinguishing the object 'for' each type of love. *Philia* is 'love for the like' and *agape* is 'love for the different.' In both cases divine love evokes a response from the Other. In *philia* the giving of love necessitates a returning of the gift. The *agape* of *creatio originalis* results in a giving of love that cannot be returned by the Other. The *agape* of incarnation is a giving of love that demands a sacrifice of the Other in light of the promise of *theosis*. In none of these cases is humanity's relation to God conceived of in a love where God and creation are with one another. For Moltmann, creation's difference is a threat/invitation to God and God's sameness is a threat/invitation to creation. In the end, from the one direction the threat is alleviated by the relaxing of boundaries and all is well in the necessary love of *philia*. And in the other direction the invitation is announced by the emphasis on boundaries made in the free love of *agape*.

In emphasizing the inclusivity of divine love for Moltmann, McDougall seems to suggest that in Moltmann's later thought God's love is more unified than the distinction between *philia* and *agape* indicates.[13] McDougall's emphasis on *agape* as the unifying motif of Moltmann is, of course, crucially important. However, she does this by downplaying, bracketing, or even dismissing the fact that for Moltmann, the stress on *agape* remains counterbalanced/contradicted by his stress on *philia*, as is indicated by his argument that in God's self-glorification there is "a contradiction or reversal of love" (*COG* 326) in God himself. In the reversal, essential self-love must become creative love for the other, that is to say selfless love. If essential self-love is *philia* and creative love is *agape*, divine love encounters the Other in two fundamentally different ways and in different directions. Moltmann maintains that eternal love is "turned" (*SL* 137ff.) in different directions—within the Trinity (*perichoresis*) and towards the world (kenosis). This implies that, for Moltmann, the very notions of kenosis and *perichoresis* rely upon a basic difference of *philia* and *agape* that cannot be lost if Moltmann's trinitarian perspective is consistent. Moltmann's unity is a contradictory unity, as we have been arguing throughout this thesis. In other words, McDougall's analysis has a one-sided quality that does not do justice to the complexity of his position. While Moltmann may not directly address the distinction between *philia* and *agape* in much of his later work, it is essential to his position.

We have seen that Moltmann goes back and forth between arguing that: 1) in the differentiation of creation from God, creation was forsaken; and 2) being forsaken is part of the process of identification. Hence, the unity in Moltmann's thinking comes as a result of his holding opposite states of affairs in tension with one another. The tension is fundamental to the dynamic concept of God that Moltmann offers as he distances himself

---

13. See McDougall, *Pilgrimage of Love*, 44ff.

from any understanding of God as one who "'is' all at one and in one" (*TH* 28). He wants neither the "god of Parmenides" nor the God of monotheism, because in both conceptions the emphasis on a static nature produces a solitary, undifferentiated individual with whom a relationship is impossible. To gain a more vibrant nature for God, and thereby all of reality, the idea of a shared divine substance is overthrown. In its place Moltmann stresses relationality (*perichoresis*), which honors difference-in-identity.

To say that Moltmann honors difference and relationality is not to deny the fundamental stress on unity—and even the ultimate privileging of unity—in his thought. His cosmogony is built on cosmic opposition. Understanding reality in terms of a basic contradiction of difference, which nevertheless yields unity, has deep roots in western thought. We can bring the vitality of this position into greater focus by looking at the connections between Moltmann's thought and its historical precedents.

Contradictory Harmonic Monism

Moltmann's thought is replete, as we have repeatedly noticed, with unity-in-opposition: diversity/unity, dissimilarity/similarity, present/future, forsakenness/indwelling, *creatio originalis/creatio nova, agape/philia, annihilation/fulfillment,* and *tragedy/feast.* Indeed, I am suggesting that his complex thought comes into coherent and fruitful focus when seen as a cosmic coincidence of opposites—a contradictory monism. Diverging motifs and contradictory assertions do not necessarily point to logical inconsistency or confusion. Indeed, contradictory assertions can be consistent and coherent when they are employed to articulate what is taken to be the fundamental contradictory constitutional make-up of the cosmos.

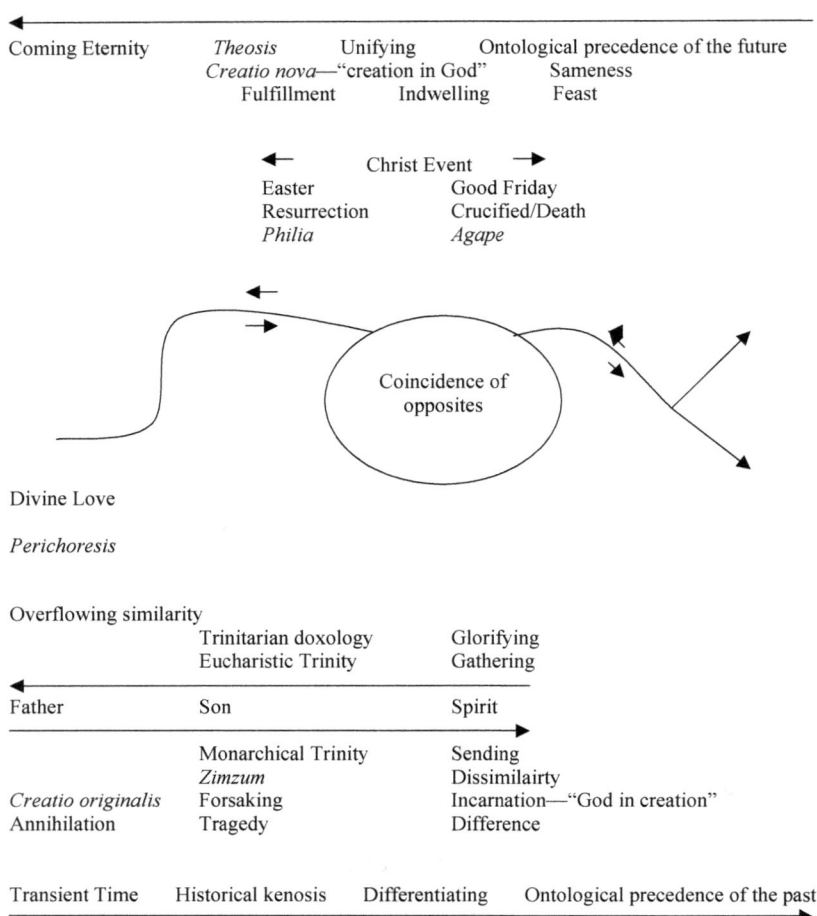

Figure 5

For Moltmann's contradictory monism reality is caught up in a "cosmic process (that) is inherently contradictory and eternally recurring."[14] There are two horizontal currents continually and simultaneously running counter to each other. Concurrently, "the universal cosmic law realizes itself in a process of differentiation" even as "there is the process in the opposite direction of a return to the universal origin and unity."[15] At the same time, the "turning point" of history is the Christ event: The crucified and risen Jesus is the *coincidentia oppositorium*. In the cross of Christ

14. Olthuis, *Models*, 29.
15. Ibid.

everything returns to God. God takes "[e]vil, sin, and rejection on himself, and in the sacrifice of his infinite love transform[s] it into goodness, grace, and election" (*SL* 212).

While other commentators have not referred to Moltmann's cosmogony as a contradictory monism—aside from Nicholas Ansell, whose recent exhaustive study also describes Moltmann's thought as contradictory/harmonic monism[16]—many have noted the similarities between Moltmann's thought and other thinkers of contradiction such as Hegel. Douglas Schuurman's interpretation of Moltmann can be a helpful guide here. In his reading both discontinuity and continuity are recognized as having a role. There is no radical departure within Moltmann; instead, the "emphasis on the continuity of creation is a theme that Moltmann maintains in his more recent books . . ."[17] But the theme of discontinuity is always countered by continuity. In his thorough examination Schuurman exposes Moltmann's view of the eschaton as a coincident of opposites. A section of one of his articles exploring Moltmann's thought is aptly entitled, "Eschaton as Fulfillment and Annihilation of Creation."[18] The "and" between fulfillment and annihilation in the title is very instructive. Schuurman shows the complexity of Moltmann's thought by focusing on the way in which Moltmann concurrently holds two opposing descriptions of eschatological creation in tension. The working assumption for Schuurman's reading of Moltmann is that the eschaton is, at the same time, both a realization of original creation and a radical overcoming of the boundaries of that creation. Creation becomes itself by ceasing to be itself.

Other critics of Moltmann have picked up on the importance of simultaneous negation and fulfillment in the structure of his thought. The similarity between Moltmann's view of reality and a Hegelian model of reality has been noted by several commentators.[19] Such a connection helps to confirm our suspicion regarding Moltmann's dynamic ontology,

---

16. See Ansell, *The Annihilation of Hell*, for his analysis of Moltmann's monism. See also Walsh, "Theology of Hope," for his sustained argument regarding the structure of Moltmann's thought.

17. Schuurman, "Creation, Eschaton, and Ethics," 48. Volf takes Schuurman's reading of Moltmann to task for not taking "more seriously [Moltmann's] stress on continuity between creation and the eschaton" ("Eschaton, Creation, and Social Ethics," 136 n. 15).

18. Ibid., 47.

19. Blocher surmises that when Moltmann suggests a "Trinity interpreted as the 'history of God' and based on the man Jesus, Jesus *qua* man as the second Person," his thought has "unmistakably Hegelian features" ("Immanence and Transcendence," 112). He suggests Moltmann appeals to Hegel as an attempt "to solve the theodicy problem after Auschwitz" (ibid.).

as Hegel has been understood as a prototype of contradictory/harmonic monism.[20] Milbank, noting the difficulty of finding difference in *creatio nova*, argues that Moltmann's view of the relationship between God and creation ultimately portrays creation as merely a stage in the development of God. Milbank explains this movement by arguing that "his effectively tritheistic perspective permits him to take in a full, 'mythological' sense, the separation of Father from Son in the dereliction of the cross, and this is integrated with his developmentalism in so far as Moltmann presents the creation as a necessary, primordial suffering which must be passed through by both God and humanity."[21] "Thus," Milbank concludes, "the Hegelian theme of a necessary alienation is still incorporated by Moltmann."[22]

Milbank's analysis is not unique here. In his analysis of Moltmann's view of the Trinity, Molnar categorizes it as a "Protestant Hegelian solution."[23] Likewise, Griffioen notes the connection between Hegel's speculative Good Friday and Moltmann's understanding of the death and resurrection of Jesus Christ.[24] It is not a large step then to conclude with Jansen that "at the heart of Moltmann's view of God lies this Hegelian dialectic."[25]

Jansen explains, "(o)ntologically, dialectic affirms the reality of the other, of what is different from oneself."[26] However, "the hallmark of a dialectical cosmogony is openness to the other in order that one may come to self-fulfillment and completion of oneself."[27] In spite of its

20. See Seerveld, "Biblical Wisdom Underneath," for the connections he makes between thinkers in this strand.

21. Milbank, "The Second Difference," 221.

22. Ibid., 223.

23. Molnar, "The Function of the Immanent Trinity," 387.

24. Moltmann discusses Hegel's idea of the speculative Good Friday in *TH* 211. Griffioen, in "G. W. F. Hegel," analyzes Hegel's use of the speculative Good Friday and the historical necessity of secularization and its implications for theology, especially in the work of Moltmann. Another helpful work in understanding Hegel on this point is Hessen, *Hegel's Trinitätslehre*.

Peters summarizes Moltmann's answer to this question: "It is the God who is love and who suffers because of this love who is revealed to us in scripture" (*God as Trinity*, 57).

25. Jansen, *Relationality*, 113. See also Geertsma's argument in *Van boven naar voren* that Moltmann's view of faith is "severely constricted—indeed is in danger of turning into a mere intellectual construction— by the very way it is accounted for intellectually using the tools of philosophy" (321). Powell offers a counter argument when he differentiates between God suffering with the world and God being dependent upon the world (*The Trinity*, 251ff.).

26. Jansen, *Relationality*, 113.

27. Ibid., 114.

affirmation of difference/plurality, the dialectic ultimately ends up giving privilege to unity.

Privileging Unity

It is noteworthy that recent postmodern critics of Hegel have also wondered if difference and plurality are adequately honored in Hegel's thought. For example, in Mark Taylor's consideration of Hegel's dialectic, he reveals the dominant role played by unity/sameness. He shows that Hegel's stress on the negation of the negation, which is characteristic of a unity-in-opposition position, still manifests a preference for unity. Despite Hegel's insistence, Taylor argues, that he is trying to reconcile identity and difference as well as union and non-union, "he consistently privileges identity and unity at the expense of difference and non-union."[28] At this point, Kelly Oliver's trenchant comment on Hegel comes to mind. In commenting on Kristeva's reading of Hegel, Oliver points out that in Hegel "negativity takes place within the One . . . Hegel's account erases rupture. The synthesis always, and in the end, emphasizes unity over crisis. For Hegel, negativity always collapses into unity and the unstable process that produces the unity is covered up."[29]

In identifying the underlying structure of Moltmann's thought as Hegelian, Milbank and others have given us a clue on how to read the fundamental tensions present in Moltmann's thought. And the postmodern critics of Hegel have helped us clarify our suspicions about the role of difference/plurality in Moltmann's dialectic. In our reading of his account of the relationship between God and creation as a form of contradictory/harmonic monism, we have established why questions regarding rupture and unity keep appearing. As we have seen, the rupture of the godforsakenness and sin of creation take place within the yet-to-be-fully-realized unity of inner-trinitarian relationships. Here as in Hegel, the "synthesis" of eschatological fulfillment emphasizes unity. For Moltmann, "being forsaken by God" is from eternity at the heart of God and at the beginning of creation. Likewise, being redeemed and reconciled by God is equiprimordially built-in to the dynamics of the Trinity and creation.[30] The godforsakenness of creation is validated and invalidated simultaneously by its fail-safe destiny in being "full-filled life" (*CG* 291) in which God

---

28. Taylor, "Denegating God," 598.

29. Oliver, *Reading Kristeva*, 42.

30. Schwöbel contends that the cross of Jesus and the Trinity are intrinsically related in Moltmann (*Trinitarian Theology Today*, 28ff.).

is all-in-all. The movement of self-differentiation is simultaneously and inherently partnered and opposed by the movement of self-identification.

In other words, whereas, in my reading of the Gospel, redemption is the surprising gift occasioned and necessitated by the fall, for Moltmann redemption as re-integration is a necessary part and parcel of the cosmic machinery, irrespective of the Fall, from the beginning. For him creation is, for the sake of redemption, ordained to move along its path, which inherently includes the cross and resurrection of Jesus Christ. "The son of God did not become man simply because of the sin" (*TK* 116). *Creatio orginalis* with its historical transitions was destined from the beginning to be overcome (rather than restored or renewed) in the redeemed *creation nova*. Despite Moltmann's strong faith affirmation of sin's rupture, his theological conceptualization in the end serves to bracket, defuse, and even erase the radical rupture of sin.[31] The incarnation is not only, or even in the first place, God's redemptive response to a creation lost through sin; its central significance is that revelation and creation are other than God and require eschatological re-integration with God. In the Sabbath Feast of Redemption "the Creator no longer remains over against his creation" (*COG* 295).

---

31. As Gunton observes, by trying to redeem evil Moltmann implants it in the life of God in spite of his motivation to keep God from being responsible for evil (*The Promise of Trinitarian Theology*, 21ff.).

CHAPTER 6

The Ethics of Discipleship

Fellowship in the Trinity

NOW THAT WE HAVE obtained an understanding of the fundamental features of Moltmann's contradictory/harmonic monism, we are in a position to examine the ethical thrust of his cosmic *perichoresis*. Moltmann's development of a Christian ethic is founded upon the ontological (dis)similarity between the perichoretic community and creation. Only in *agape*'s creation of connections between divine life and human/creational life by 'contradicting the contradiction' does a positive ethic become knowable.[1] Yet, it must be remembered that any comparison of God and creation in Moltmann is preceded and made possible by an initial radical difference between God and creation. The comparison between Creator and creature is precluded until God himself allows the comparison in the giving of himself.[2] In God's revelation of himself, creation's difference from the Creator gives way as a relationship of correspondence emerges. In this chapter we will examine Moltmann's ethic, his conception of kenosis in particular, which develops as *philia*'s relationship of correspondence take shapes in contrast to *agape*'s relationship of opposition.

Divine Life as the Source for Ethics

Redemptive *agape* encounters a sinful humanity in the midst of a forsaken creation. As the incarnate and abandoned Christ reveals God to creation,

---

1. Volf makes the connection between the priority given the eschaton over creation in relationship to ethics when he argues that when ethical behaviour is oriented "to the structures of original creation as opposed to their various distortions through sin" the effect is to take "eschatology out of ethics, indeed positively barring eschatology from social ethics" ("Eschaton, Creation, and Social Ethics," 137). See also Jones, *Transformed Judgment*.

2. Pannenberg's differentiation between religious experience and "the natural theology of philosophy" is helpful in understanding Moltmann here (*Systematic Theology*, 1:107ff.).

"the principle of fellowship is fellowship with those who are different
. . ." (*CG* 28). In this act, the perichoretic community invites the different Other into the divine fellowship. Once the fellowship of God and creation is established through kenosis an analogy of relationality between divine life and creaturely life is posited.[3] Difference must precede similarity, as "the basis and starting point of analogy is this dialectic" (ibid.) wherein God is revealed in his opposite. And it is on the basis of this God-knowledge that it is possible to speak again of the relationship of the human creature to the Creator.[4]

Here the characteristic tension present between forsaken creation and God is evident. Ethics for Moltmann arises out of the confrontation with humanity by God's self-revelation. The use of the Trinity to set the basic direction in the development of a Christian ethic is consistent with the ontological tendencies we have uncovered. Moltmann clearly makes the link between divine life and ethics when he asserts, "because in the systems and dogmatics of Christian theology the understanding of God was always normative for the understanding of human beings and the world, I began my contributions with this apparently abstract and remote theme of the doctrine of the Trinity and developed a social doctrine of the Trinity" (*HTG* 181).

For Moltmann there is an indisputable tie between a doctrine of God and a doctrine of creation, which then leads to an ethic.[5] In his consideration of Barth, Moltmann declares that "Barth's doctrine of the Trinity is the blueprint of his doctrine of creation" (*HTG* 130). Moltmann goes on to conclude that "anyone who thinks that this or that part of the structure of his doctrine of creation has to be changed must therefore be in a position to change his doctrine of the Trinity" (ibid.). Here Moltmann outlines the progression of his work. First was his rethinking of the doctrine of the Trinity in terms of *perichoresis*. Following the use of reciprocity in describing the interior life of God, Moltmann reconsidered the relationship between God and creation, using kenosis/*agape* and *theosis*/*philia* to describe the interactions between the divine community and the creaturely

---

3. Compare with Levinas, *Of God who Comes to Mind*, 3ff., wherein he describes ethics as an interrupting force that out of the encounter with the Other. Love for Levinas is understood more in terms of desire than a replication of relations. As a result, ethics for Levinas seems more creational than metaphysical.

4. An excellent example of trinitarian ethics rooted in Moltmann's approach is Volf, *After Our Likeness*.

5. Of course, Moltmann's theology of hope frames his understanding of ethics. See Genovesi's treatment of this relationship in *Expectant Creativity*.

Other. In this next step, the interplay between the concurrent movements between God and creation are used to develop an ethics of discipleship.

It follows that creation as originally forsaken cannot provide the basis for ethics. To attempt to do so is preemptive. Rather, only in God's revelation of the divine community in Jesus Christ do the norms for creational life become manifest. In the crucified and risen Jesus Christ inner-trinitarian life is established as the analogue to creaturely life. The analogy manifests that "the ethic of discipleship is the true consequence of the revelation of the Father of Jesus Christ. The ethics of discipleship matches the trinitarian understanding of the Father" (*HTG* 16). It is only God's absence/presence in *creatio originalis* that can serve as a source for morality, not creation itself. Creation is merely a parable or an image of the new creation. As we have seen, there is no goodness or source of order to be found in forsaken creation. Hence, the overcoming of creation's (dis)order by the work of Jesus Christ is the necessary condition for a life of discipleship.

The overcoming of creation's (dis)order is evident in Moltmann's view of humanity as eschatologically oriented. Human nature is teleologically oriented as it is designed to move from *imago Dei* to *gloria Dei*.[6] The continuity/discontinuity of the human being in this process of transformation guides Moltmann's ethics: "human beings are *imago Trinitas* in their personal fellowship with one another" (*GC* 241). Moltmann's distinction here parallels the earlier clarification regarding the relationship between *creatio originalis*, *creatio nova*, *creatio continua*, and the eternal Sabbath. In the *creatio originalis*, a human being is *imago Dei,* which "is the original designation of human beings" (*GC* 215). This is distinct from the *imago Christi* of the *creatio nova*, which is "the messianic calling of human beings" (ibid.), and the *gloria Dei est homo* in the "eschatological glorification of human beings" (ibid.) in the final *perichoresis* of God and creation.

In other words, human relations are, in the end, to embody the perichoretic nature of trinitarian relationships. Just as Moltmann understands the divine nature as vibrant, he also sees human nature as dynamic. Eschatologically understood, human beings are in transition from an original state of closed selves who have been abandoned to their own devices to full membership in the giving relations of trinitarian life. This transition of humanity from forsaken to fulfilled depends upon God in Christ 'contradicting the contradiction' and founding the analogy between divine life and creational life that allows the reproduction of divine *perichoresis* among the already fallen human community.

6. Compare with Pannenberg's discussion of human persons in *Systematic Theology*, 1:430ff.

Analogy of Relationality

The analogy between God and humanity can be understood as an analogy of relationality (*analogia relationis*). Relationality has a two-fold meaning in this context. First, it refers to the "how" of the analogy. In Moltmann's dialectic of reconciliation, as evidenced by the notion of a godforsaken creation, disconnection is prior to connection in the relationship between God and creation. The difference between God and creation is so radical that no correspondences can be legitimately drawn by humanity until God overcomes the gap. Only from a relationship of difference between God and humanity can an analogy develop in which correspondences are drawn.

Second, relationality refers to the "what" of the analogy. In the giving of himself to creation in the overcoming of the disconnection, God reveals himself to be essentially relational. God is not merely relational in his dealings with creation, but also within himself; God is community. The content of God's self-revelation is that the Godhead is a threesome of Others who share a fundamental sameness eternally involved in self-giving and self-receiving. The result is a divine community formed through the intimate indwelling of each Other. In the giving of himself in Jesus Christ, God not only reveals the inner-trinitarian divine relations, but also establishes that divine relationality is to be the model for all relationality. The relationship between same Others is perfectly exemplified in the perichoretic exchange between members of the Trinity. This ideal of perfect self-giving and self-receiving becomes the ethical norm for human inter-subjectivity.

The norm is elucidated by Moltmann's description of the connection between the divine community and the human community: "the Trinity corresponds to a community in which people are defined through their relations with one another and in their significance for one another, not in opposition to one another, in terms of power and possession" (*TK* 198). The analogy between the divine community and the human community does not begin with an understanding of *perichoresis* as perfected human mutuality. Rather, establishing the analogy is dependent on a primary radical difference between our creational experience of relationality and the perichoretic relations of the Trinity. The violence and selfishness that characterize forsaken humanity's relationships are the opposite of the vulnerability and kenosis of divine relationships. Moltmann does not understand the norm for human relationality to be an extrapolation from imperfect human community to a perfect divine community; rather, the revelation of inner-trinitarian life contradicts the barrenness of present experience with "the model for a just and livable community in the world of nature and human beings" (*HTG* xiii).

The Penetration/Overflowing of Creation

Any remnant of relationality that remains within forsaken humanity's relationality does not suffice as a comparison to the overflowing love existing in divine relations. It is only "in so far as God is revealed in his opposite, [that] he can be known by the Godless and those who are abandoned by God, and it is this knowledge which brings them into correspondence with God and . . . enables them even to have the hope of being like God" (*CG* 27). The ideal of *perichoresis* can only be known when God penetrates the forsakenness and allows creation to experience his fellowship.[7] The incarnation of Jesus Christ shows God's faithfulness, inasmuch as he willingly subjects himself to the conditions of *creatio originalis* and the actualization of the *nihil* within creation. The forsaking of creation is simultaneously validated and invalidated by the cross of Jesus. Both abandonment and violence are overcome by the faithfulness of the Father in Jesus Christ. The cycle of violence is broken through its active acceptance and the refusal to respond with vengeance. Through his willingness to endure pain, "God's faithfulness to his creatures is manifested as his indestructible love which overcomes a world in conflict" (*HTG* 52). Just as in the Trinity "the divine persons are there for one another in their mutual Others," so also "on the cross of Christ this love is there for Others, the sinners, those in conflict, enemies" (*HTG* 53). The cross is "an action which takes up all who believe in him into the eternal life of the divine life" (ibid.).

Yet the atonement accomplished in the cross and resurrection not only counters the actualized *nihil*, but also the conditions of the original creation. Furthermore, atonement is not only for the oppressed. Atonement comes also for the oppressors, "from the mercy of the Father through the God-forsakenness which the Son endures as a representative in the unburdening power of the Holy Spirit. A single movement of love arises out of the pain of the Father, is manifest in the suffering of the Son and is experienced in the Spirit of life . . . His justice justifies the unjust" (ibid.). In this justification of the unjust, *agape* is manifest as something

---

7. The re-filling of creation leads to Schuurman's concern: "My chief objection to Moltmann's eschatology and ethics is that his vision of the eschaton includes an unwarranted annihilation of creation, resulting in an ethic that is inadequate with respect to valuations and moral directives that affirm creaturely life . . . How does the object of Christian hope 'guide obedience in love on to the path towards earthly, corporeal, social reality'" ("Creation, Eschaton, and Ethics," 43).

new, for "in order to live with the past it is not enough just to atone for past guilt" (ibid.). Rather, "something new must be created so that 'the old has passed away'" (ibid.). Divine love as *agape* is able to bear the suffering of both victim and perpetrator and transform isolation into community.

Being brought into the divine fellowship gives humanity this radically different model of relationality that it is to embody as,

> "The unity of the community is in truth the trinitarian fellowship of God himself, of which it is a reflection and in which it participates. This fellowship with the Trinity and in the Trinity is held out to the community of the disciples because it is grounded in the prayer of Jesus, which the community is certain is heard by the Father. The community is the 'lived out' Trinity. In the community, that mutual love is practiced that corresponds to the eternal love of the Trinity" (*HTG* 63).

The confrontation of the forsaken self by God as different (incarnate) Other prompts the repentance and reorientation of the self as God makes himself known. In being grasped by the revelation of the Other, the self becomes aware of the obligation demanded.[8] The in-breaking of God's self-revelation is not to be understood only in light of its faith-oriented qualification, but also in terms of its ethical consequences.[9] Here *agape* contradicts all the conditions of forsakenness. In *agape*, Jesus' humanity stands in judgment against the self unto itself for the sake of the self. When the self's experience of separation is faced with the difference of the trinitarian community as revealed in Jesus, the language of the self as unto itself is replaced with the language of the self towards another. God gives himself to the forsaken Other in and through Jesus Christ. In the midst of the actualized *nihil* God's fundamental disposition towards humanity is kenotic. Through God's kenosis for forsaken creation divine love must become *agape*, for here we find the power of (re)connection and (re)creation.[10]

---

8. Ward, in "The Revelation of the Holy Other," compares Barth to Levinas on this point, with links to Moltmann. He states: "In revelation the I discovers itself obliged, already in service to the Other" (167). For an interesting discussion of the discovery of obligation without revelation, see Caputo, *Against Ethics*, 6–19.

9. Ward is again helpful on this point in "The Revelation of the Holy Other." He talks about revelation resulting in a rethinking of the theological and anthropological grammar that produces "new grammars of self and God" (168).

10. Ward points out that in Barth "kenosis is the fundamental operation of the Trinity" (ibid.). Jüngel, in *The Doctrine of the Trinity*, has shown that it is this divine self-giving which is the ontological basis of Barth's *analogia relationas*. The *analogia relationis* is "founded on the doctrine of the Trinity by the proposition of the *perichoresis* of the three divine modes of being" (68).

The possibility of God's self-communication, and thereby (re)creation, is founded upon the pervasive giving of the self present in trinitarian life. In the reconciling revelation of himself, God has revealed himself as Trinity. And as Trinity, God must be conceived of as relational, as the members mutually indwell and dwell with one another. The giving of God's self to humanity is revealed to be parallel to and rooted in the giving of the self of each member of the Godhead to each Other. The perichoretic nature of God is constant. *Perichoresis* as *philia* among the members of the Trinity precedes the giving of revelation of Jesus Christ to humanity. In being directed towards forsaken humanity, trinitarian *perichoresis* discloses itself as *agape*. In this giving *agape* is not only the source of the revelation, but also the content of it. God as community reveals that we too are to be kenotic selves towards one another. The first step in becoming the glory of God is for humanity to practice *agape* and experience living under the obligation of giving to and receiving from the Other.

Imago Christi

A (dis)similarity between God and creation is argued for in the analogy of relationality. Through humanity's "face-to-face" relation with God, the divine community is revealed to be the pattern for the community of creation. Jesus Christ is the nexus between the divine community and the community of creation.[11] Through his kenotic sacrifice on the cross for the sake of the community of creation, Jesus Christ manifests the overabundant love of divine *perichoresis*. The idea of *perichoresis* that unfolds in Moltmann's doctrine of the Trinity becomes the significant concept for his ethics as he refines the assertion of the Trinity as the social program of humanity. Ethics takes its departure from "a perichoretic doctrine of the Trinity [that] entails that the levels of relationship in *perichoresis* and mutuality within the Trinity, rather than the levels of constitution within the Trinity, are normative for the relationship of God to creation and all the corresponding relationships in creation" (*HTG* 132). The results of making central the notion of *perichoresis* are the same for the doctrine of creation as they were for the doctrine of God: just as "the concept of community, mutuality, *perichoresis*, comes to the foreground in the un-

---

11. Meeks explains, "Moltmann maintained that the resurrection is not already the eschatological fulfillment of reconciliation. Rather it points beyond itself to something not yet realized or present . . . Thus for Moltmann, the event of the cross and resurrection creates a real process of reconciliation. Thus history . . . will be conceived as open to the coming reconciliation in the 'future of Christ' in God's kingdom. A christologically shaped view of history will be in fact eschatological" (*Origins*, 98).

derstanding of God, and takes up, relativizes and limits the concept of one-sided rule, then the understanding of the determination of human beings among each other and their relationship to nature also changes" (*HTG* 181). From this basis, Moltmann can assert, "our starting point here is that all relationships which are analogous to God reflect the primal, reciprocal indwelling and mutual interpenetration of the trinitarian *perichoresis*" (*GC* 17). He finds "the Christian doctrine of the Trinity provides the intellectual means whereby to harmonize personality and sociality in the community of men and women, without sacrificing the one to the other" (*TK* 199).

The forsaken Other who repents and expresses faith in Jesus Christ as a result of this confrontation begins her walk along the way of Jesus Christ, as "the confession of Jesus as the Christ also involves a practical discipleship that follows the messianic path his own life took; and that means an ethic which has to be made identifiably Christian" (*WJC* 118). For Moltmann, ethics is distinctively Christian as an "ethics of discipleship." "So what today's dispute over the Christian nature of Christian ethics is really about," argues Moltmann, "is nothing less than the messiahship of Jesus" (ibid.). This serious challenge to make ethics identifiably Christian is a primary concern: "Christian ethics are not asked merely for good or better solutions to general problems. They are asked how far the way of Jesus is to be taken seriously" (ibid.). And Moltmann goes on to explain why this has become such a pressing concern today. We can see that "in a 'post-Christian' society, and especially in the deadly contradictions into which the modern social system has brought humanity and the earth, the special and identifiable Christian ethic of the discipleship of Jesus makes itself publicly evident" (ibid.). Within this context, "faith in Christ can no longer be separated from ethics" (ibid.). The comprehensive nature of understanding of Christ as the Lord and Redeemer of all of life "means that christology and christopraxis become one, so that a total, holistic knowledge of Christ puts its stamp not only on the mind and the heart, but on the whole life in the community of Christ . . ." (*WJC* 119). The experience of faith in Jesus Christ leads to following his messianic way.

The believer's call within fallen creation is to be *imago Christi*. As image of Christ, we are obligated to practice *agape* and to be involved in the transforming process whereby isolation becomes community and oppression becomes fellowship. Even human *agape* can renew. The life of renewal, which involves both receiving and giving, is linked with the traditional theological categories of justification, sanctification, and glorification.[12] Being the *imago Christi* happens during the in-between time for the believer: "Between the experienced justification of the sinner and the hoped-for glorification of the person justified lies the path of sanctification, which has to do with 'putting on the new human being, created after the likeness of God" (*GC* 227). This means "likeness to God is both gift and charge, indicative and imperative" (ibid.). Receiving the revelation of God as community allows the previously forsaken person to be transformed by the experience of divine love. As a result, love calls her to live as a member of a "contrast-society" (*WJC* 122), for *agape* must first establish difference before seeking similarity. The recipient of the revelation of God "comes into harmony with himself *in spe*, but into disharmony with himself *in re*" (*TH* 91). This disharmony lies not only within, but "those who hope in Christ can no longer put up with reality as it is, but begin to suffer under it, to contradict it" (*TH* 21). In the process, the person moves from being forsaken and despairing in the face of the threat of reality to identifying with and participating in the divine community. This fellowship results in a questioning of all of reality that does not reflect the ideal of *perichoresis* as trinitarian life becomes available for comparison in the analogy of relationality. And yet this questioning of forsaken creation leads to a more radical giving of oneself with the hope of all things becoming new.

As forsaken, present creation is characterized more by violence than mutuality. The Synoptic Gospels, according to Moltmann, speak to the reality of this age, which is between God's *agape* made known in Jesus Christ and the complete indwelling of creation by God in *philia*. Many of Jesus' actions are interpreted by the Gospels as examples of *agape* given to one's enemies: "the situations which Jesus keeps tackling are those of human conflict: the healthy against the sick, the rich against the poor, men against women, Pharisees against tax collectors, the good against the wicked, the perpetrators against the victims" (*HTG* 44). The context of Jesus' ministry of reconciliation is the opposition that exists between forsaken persons as "there is only the either-or of the friend-enemy relationship" (*HTG* 45). The asymmetry of power in the friend-enemy relationship can (must?) produce the dynamic of perpetrator and victim. As stronger, the perpetrator exercises power to take from the weaker while the victim is forced to submit to the desires of the Other. There is a co-dependency present in the dynamics between the powerful and the powerless as the oppressor strives for his independence through his use of the victim. As the victim is consumed, the perpetrator must search for another self from which to take

---

12. See Sponheim, *Faith and the Other*, 113ff.

in order to strive for his selfish independence. In this cycle of violence, the paradoxical situation arises where the oppressive self's search for autonomy and self-fulfillment is always dependent upon conquering an Other.

Moltmann argues that God, as manifest in Jesus Christ, is a God who executes justice for the poor and oppressed. Scripture attests to the divine protection of the weak as God chose to be one of the weak. Therefore, he asserts that anyone who wields power against the weak also wields power against the suffering God. By identifying with the victims (was not Christ a victim?) God reveals the way out of the cycle of violence. Acts against the poor and weak are re-enactments of the brutality committed against Jesus. It is "God himself (who) is the victim of the violent" (*HTG* 47). Jesus' answer was not to overpower the powerful; rather, "he himself bears the suffering of the world" (ibid.). On the cross, Jesus allowed the destructiveness of the cycle of violence to be borne out. Jesus' crucifixion is not to be understood as the origin or continuation of a cult of violence. Jesus' death was not merely for death's sake, but "by 'bearing' and enduring sins he does atonement for the victims of violence; he makes the violent repent and so restores them" (ibid.).

Responding Creatively to Violence

In the Son's death the Father took upon himself the suffering and guilt of humanity.[13] Moltmann understands Jesus' cross and resurrection, and its Old Testament anticipations, as a creative response to violence. In the crucified Christ, the oppressed find solidarity with God. Christ is revealed as the one who "brings eternal communion with God and God's life-giving righteousness through his passion into the passion story of this world and identifies God with the victims of violence" (*HTG* 48). There is a community between God and the oppressed as "Christ experienced and suffered our distress so that we might experience his brotherhood in our distress" (ibid.). Experiencing community with God means that the oppressed have "divine protection" (ibid.).

Though God identifies with the poor and the victim, it is important to remember that both the perpetrator and the victim are affected when violence is committed. Moltmann describes the effect by saying, "Violence destroys life on both sides, but in different ways: on the one side through evil and on the Other through suffering" (*HTG* 49). Usually, it is not difficult to discern one's own suffering. Yet, suffering is not always vis-

---

13. See Volf's summary of Moltmann's identification of victims with God in *Exclusion and Embrace*, 22ff.

ible to Others. Describing the inability of perpetrators to see the result of their violent actions, Moltmann says, "the liberation of the perpetrators of violence from their injustice is not self-evident in most cases, at any rate not for the violent who gain from their injustice. They do not see the sufferings they cause their victims. They are blinded" (ibid.). Both the powerlessness of the victim and the blindness of the perpetrator point to the necessity of "the way to freedom and justice" beginning on both sides so that "the liberation of the oppressed from the suffering of oppression calls for the liberation of the oppressors from the injustice of oppression" (ibid.). In Christ, God atones for both the guilt of perpetrators and the sufferings of the oppressed.[14] Just as the oppressed find protection, rights, and community, the oppressors find judgment, forgiveness and the offer of fellowship.

The path to Christ is different for the victim and the perpetrator as there is a difference between God's righteousness that "justifies" and God's justice which "executes justice" (*HTG* 46). The one who "executes justice" is the one who both brings judgment and "puts the weak and the vulnerable under his protection" (*HTG* 47). The bringing of this justice results in an identification: "Anyone who violates the weak, the vulnerable violates [God]" (ibid.). Executing justice, then, implies "God's preferential option for the poor" (ibid.). The suffering of the victim becomes God's suffering and "Christ brings eternal communion with God and God's life-giving righteousness" (*HTG* 48). Nonetheless, God also acts with a justifying righteousness that leads to atonement, taking the punishment deserved by the perpetrator upon himself. Here God's favor is not reserved for "the poor" but Christ's atonement "reconciles the hostile, sinful world" (*HTG* 47). As loving and merciful, God's "justice justifies the unjust" (*HTG* 53).

The promise of forgiveness is very important for the perpetrator because she knows "that injustice can never be undone" (*HTG* 49). Forgiveness can relieve the despairing guilt. There is need for forgiveness as it is guilt that further dehumanizes the perpetrator by either creating the autonomous, self-justifying self or by destroying one's self-respect. In either case, the perpetrator becomes further removed from connection with the Other. Moltmann maintains, "there is no liberation from guilt without atonement!" (*HTG* 50). However, "atonement is not a human possibility, but only a divine one" (ibid.). Only God can enact atonement as "a power which liberates perpetrators and their descendants from

---

14. As Wiebe summarizes, "the gospel is not aimed just at reversing the pecking order but toward bringing the whole relationship of oppressor and oppressed to an end" ("Revolution," 109).

self-hatred and enables them to live in peace" (*HTG* 49). In the biblical narrative it is only God who has the power to bear the sins of his people. Because "violence . . . against God's creatures is always also a violation of God himself" (*HTG* 50), God's love is violated when evil is done. If it is God's love that is violated, then "God must bear and sustain the pain of his love" (ibid.). Sustaining his love means that God "overcome[s] his wrath by rising above the pain which is added to it" (ibid.). In the atoning process God "transforms human guilt into divine suffering by bearing human sin" (ibid.). Divine suffering is rooted in excessive, creative love. In the bearing of sin, God creates mercy out of wrath. Because divine love is creative, "the crucified Christ has nothing to do with a God of vengeance or a divine punitive judge" (*HTG* 51). Jesus Christ taking upon himself the suffering of sin and the Father answering with mercy accomplishes atonement. "Atonement is . . . the form of suffering taken by the love of God for this world," argues Moltmann, as "the love of God wounded by human injustice and violence becomes the love of God which endures pain, and the 'wrath of God' becomes divine mercy" (ibid.).

Embodying Creative Love to the Violent Other

God's righteousness is not a distributive justice but a creative justice.[15] This righteousness is rooted in God's *agape* love that creates in difference. The community of believers, those following the ethics of discipleship, is called to embody this creative love, even in the face of evil. Within the community of believers "mutual love is practiced which corresponds to the eternal love of the Trinity" (*HTG* 64). For Moltmann the confession of Christ involves the manifestation of the perichoretic love of the Trinity. This unselfish gift of oneself is to be given even when the recipient is the perpetrator of violence. Christian ethics is a constant asking of the question, "how far is the way of Jesus to be taken seriously" (*WJC* 118)? The totality of commitment to Christ results in following the way of Christ in the whole of life. As Jesus Christ has shown, in our brokenness this means living kenotically, excessively giving oneself to the Other. This is what Jesus Christ has revealed to humanity. Moltmann explains, "taking the Sermon on the Mount seriously and following Christ go together" (*WJC* 126). In the Sermon on the Mount, "everything depends on 'doing'" (ibid.). Moltmann holds that the expectations of the Sermon on the Mount are not to be understood as "unreasonable," but the community of believers must work to fulfill it. Any attempt to deny the validity of the Sermon on

---

15. See also Moltmann and Kung, *The Ethics of World Religions*.

the Mount for today "mocks God," "says that Jesus is wrong," and "does not know God the Creator" (*WJC* 127). The fulfilling of the Sermon on the Mount requires excessive giving of one's self for the sake of the Other. In the face of violence, the response of a follower of Jesus Christ is still to be kenotic. For it is only in the "renunciation of violence" (*WJC* 129) given by kenosis that the "vicious circle of violence and counter-violence is broken" (ibid.). To react through self-assertion would deny the possibility of reconciliation as "counter-violence supplies evil with its supposed justification, and often stabilizes it" (ibid.). Giving oneself to the violent Other "shows up the absurdity of evil" (ibid.).

Just as the sending of the Son was not motivated by God's need for retribution, but by his desire for community with creation, the exposure of oneself to violence is not the goal, but a step towards the goal of reconciliation with the offender. "So even 'the renunciation of violence,'" argues Moltmann, "is only a negative paraphrase of the conquest of violence through the non-violent creation of peace" (ibid.). The love that motivates acts of non-violence has a desire not merely for the absence of violence, but also for taking "responsibility for our enemies" (*WJC* 130). The hope revealed in the giving of oneself to the point of suffering is the freeing of the violent Other, because "liberating power is inherent in vicarious suffering too" (ibid.). The intent is to change from a power-over relationship to a perichoretic sharing. Only through the self's kenosis, following the way of Jesus, is the path towards redemption of the perpetrator possible.

Peace cannot be achieved through the annihilation of those with whom we disagree or from whom we are in some sense disconnected. The reliance upon violence, potential or realized, to maintain peace breeds a false security. The dynamic of power-over is still at work. Lasting peace can only be achieved through "neighborly love" (ibid.). By escaping the cycle of violence and its call to react, the person of peace can create something new. To love our enemies is an act of "creative love" (*WJC* 131). This new relationship embodies God's *agape* love. Reacting non-violently is still attached somewhat to the cycle of violence as a re-action. The final step in moving beyond violence is the active birthing of peace through love. Responding non-violently and creating peace are the steps taken towards reconciliation and the redemption of the perpetrator, as the question turns from "how can I protect myself, and deter my enemies from attacking me?" to "how can I deprive my enemy of his hostility?" (ibid.).

In his discussion of non-violent action, Moltmann seems to reject counter-violence as a legitimate reaction to the overpowering presence of a violent Other. Moltmann's position is that counter-violence must not be used because its use results in a loss of hope for the redemption of the enemy, and therefore the loss of community. Following Christ means the kenotic giving-up of oneself to the violence in order to break the vicious cycle. It is only through the suffering of the victim that the perpetrator may recognize the humanity that is being destroyed. Through the willing self-giving of the victim to the violent Other the absurdity of violence is revealed. In the context of violence, responsibility for the enemy (perpetrator) comes at the risk of the loss of the self. The giving-up of self-interest is the ethical thing to do, for reconciliation and peace can only be achieved by the redemption of the Other.

To live kenotically, for Moltmann, means to choose an "ethic of responsibility for our enemies" over an "ethic of self-assertion" (ibid.). In relationship to enemies, the call is to embody *agape*. As Moltmann has previously maintained, *agape* brings into existence that which is not. To respond to violence non-kenotically, that is, with counter-violence, would not be creative. The lack of creativity results in the propagation of the fallen status quo. Instead, *agape* seeks to bring new connections to life between enemies and victims. The only possibility forward towards new connections begins with the self-sacrifice of *agape*. These creative responses are to be anticipations of the new creation promised by God. Through this creative love "we draw our enemies into our own sphere of responsibility, and extend our responsibility to them" (ibid.). Self-sacrifice in *agape* is intended to do what self-assertion cannot do—establish the conditions of mutuality.

Agape leads to the possibility of a perichoretic community in which the self constantly gives to and receives from the Other. However, the sympathy of *agape* requires a constant self-giving, even if there is no reciprocity. The endless giving hopes for a return. From initial opposition, *agape* anticipates the forming of correspondences. If the enemy responds favorably to the self-gift, the *perichoresis* of redeemed inter-human relations begins to emerge. In community, *agape* flips into *philia* as out of the understanding empathy arises a connecting sympathy. The love of the enemy leads to a love of a friend as the giving of oneself kenotically to an Other leads to the reciprocating exchange between the former enemy and victim.

For Moltmann, there is an either/or of self-assertion or self-sacrifice for the self in the face of the violent Other. The only redemptive move is self-sacrifice because in this move lies the possibility of reconciliation. If the enemy responds with further violence, *agape* requires further giving. To stop giving of oneself to an enemy is to stop loving. Within the oppositional disconnection of godforsaken creation the self is obligated to the Other. To stop loving the Other, even the violent Other, is to be too self-centered.

The Power of Compassion

God's kenotic presence confronts the immorality of a forsaken creation that has realized its *nihil*. Divine life is shown to be the way of all life, even the life of a creation not yet filled with God's presence. In Moltmann's criticism of philosophical monotheism we find not only a move towards a dynamic ontology, but also its ethical pulse. The refining of the doctrine of the social Trinity suggests an ordering to the creaturely community. Human relationships are both normed and evaluated in terms of and in accordance with the social Trinity.[16] The divine community as norm allows Moltmann to evaluate critically the abuse of power for the sake of unity. If God is no longer viewed as the supreme ruler over all that is, but as a divine community, then any hierarchy, whether it is within the Trinity, between God and creation, or in creation, is challenged. Moltmann argues "the expansion of the doctrine of the Trinity in the concept of God can only really overcome this transposition of religious into political monotheism, by overcoming the notion of a universal monarchy of the one God" (*TK* 197).[17] Without this theological backing, the power-over model must look to itself for justification. Developing the perichoretic, future-oriented view of divine unity makes it "impossible to form the figure of the omnipotent, universal monarch, who is reflected in earthly rulers, out of the unity of this Father, this Son and this Spirit" (ibid.). The Father is not "the archetype of the mighty ones of this world" (ibid.). Rather, the Father is "almighty because he exposes himself to the experience of suffering, pain, helplessness and death . . . what he is is not almighty power; what he is is love" (ibid.).

The glory of God, as revealed in his suffering love, is manifest in humanity as "the glory of the triune God is reflected, not in the crowns of kings and the triumphs of victors, but in the face of the crucified Jesus, and in the faces of the oppressed whose brother he became" (*TK* 198). With the trinitarian God as the point of departure, it is no longer the powerful and privileged few who represent God, but those who are found

---

16. For discussions regarding power, political order, and the church in Moltmann, especially in relationship to the Anabaptist tradition, see Müller-Fahrenholz, *The Kingdom and the Power*; Wright, *Disavowing Constantine*; and Rasmusson, *The Church as Polis*.

17. Moltmann, in the end of *TK*, uses his conception of the Trinity to critique perceived errors in the structure of the family, the church, and the state.

living in community. Such solidarity is found in "the fellowship of believers and of the poor" (ibid.). The suffering and oppressed people are the community of Christ. The notion of the sovereign ruler has been replaced by a suffering God. God is not sitting atop the hierarchy, he is below bearing the weight as the many support the few. The doctrine of the social Trinity challenges not only institutional hierarchy; the Trinity is the social program for humanity.

Beyond *Imago Dei* through *Imago Christi* to *Imago Gloria*

God reveals true humanity to forsaken humanity by identifying himself with the suffering of forsakenness and by manifesting himself to be absolute love, not absolute power. If God himself is suffering love, then the *imago Dei* of humanity must be understood in these terms. Moltmann argues for just this connection. Humanity bears God's image when it embodies suffering love in its relationships. Divine love is revealed in godforsakenness as that love which undertakes suffering for the sake of the Other. This is the *agape* love which empties itself for the Other. The self-emptying of God in *agape* for the sake of creation, both as the divine withdrawal and the incarnation, defines a God whose "divinity . . . is kenosis" (UL 120). Through God's constant kenotic activity, the divine community opens/empties itself for the Other. It is this very opening/emptying of God for the Other which invites community-through-kenosis. And this love as self-emptying becomes the image to be born by humanity in a forsaken world. God as community-through-kenosis means that "it is not . . . the solitary individual which is thought worthy to correspond to God and participate in God's eternal being but the human fellowship of persons" (*HTG* 62). Community through self-giving overcomes self-assertion and self-determination as ideals. In this perspective, it is human fellowship that is "the image of the triune God, not just as the image of his rule but also as the image of his inner being" (*HTG* 63).

Moltmann develops, as we have emphasized, this social understanding of the *imago Dei* in terms of an analogy of relationality. To speak of a human being's likeness to God "first of all says something about the God who creates his image for himself, and who enters into a particular relationship with that image, before it says anything about the human being who is created in this form" (*GC* 220). Moltmann concludes from this assertion that "the nature of human beings springs from their relationship to God" (*GC* 220). But it must be remembered that "the true likeness to God is to be found, not at the beginning of God's history with mankind, but at its end" (*GC* 225). Only as goal is the likeness "present in that beginning and during every moment of that history" (ibid.). As godforsaken, humanity in original creation lacked God's true likeness. Humanity at creation awaited fulfillment, a fulfillment that became more difficult for God when creation actualized the *nihil* through its loss of hope. In spite of the disconnection between God and creation, the likeness of God exists as the goal. It is the promised relationship between a lacking, and therefore desiring, creation and the coming God that defines human nature. The fundamental position of creation's lack and God's promise means "the God who creates for himself his image on earth finds his correspondence in that image" (*GC* 220). From the notion of God finding his correspondence in the image that he has created, Moltmann derives his understanding that "human likeness to God consists in the fact that human beings, for their part correspond to God" (ibid.). God must empty himself for the sake of the Other in order for the Other to join the divine fellowship.

Because God corresponds to humanity and humanity to God, humanity as the image of God "becomes an indirect revelation of his divine Being in earthly form" (ibid.). As God's image, humanity participates in "three fundamental relationships: they rule over other earthly creatures as God's representatives and in his name; they are God's counterpart on earth, the counterpart to whom he wants to talk, and who is intended to respond to him; and they are the appearance of God's splendour, and his glory on earth" (*GC* 221). It is the whole existence of the person that is involved in these relationships. Yet, Moltmann maintains that "there is apparently one point at which God's relationship to human beings is manifested and can be recognized: the human face" (ibid.).[18] Divine likeness "is expressed in concentrated form in the person's face" (*GC* 222).[19]

Moltmann's contradictory dialectic is evident even in this discussion of the face. Humanity as original creation lacked something in being designated *imago Dei* and would only be perfected in the direct encounter with God. As *imago Dei*, humanity does not participate in the intimate fellowship of trinitarian life. Moltmann views the *imago Dei* as a promise pointing to the future when humanity is perfected through God's direct and complete presence.

At the same time "the human being's original designation to be God's image already implies the eschatological promise of perceiving God 'face

18. Compare Moltmann's of discussion "the face" with those of Lévinas in various works. For example, see Lévinas and Kearney, "Dialogue with Emmanuel Lévinas."

19. See Sponheim's discussion of Levinas and Moltmann on the face in *Faith and the Other*, 54ff.

to face'" (ibid.). This process is described by Moltmann: "the restoration or new creation of the likeness to God comes about in the fellowship of believers with Christ: since he is the messianic *imago Dei*, believers become *imago Christi*, and through this enter upon the path which will make them *gloria Dei* on earth" (*GC* 226). When direct fellowship with God is consummated through God's coming from the future to indwell creation, there will no longer be a need for an image because all of creation will be penetrated with his being. Moltmann understands humanity's likeness to God to be "a historical process with an eschatological termination; it is not a static condition" (*GC* 227). As caught up in the eschatological process, "*being* human [not only] means *becoming* human" (ibid.), it also means being "*gloria Dei* on earth" (*GC* 226). Human beings as the *imago Dei* concurrently point to God's partial presence in *creatio originalis* and the promise of God's overflowing presence in the future. At creation, human beings did not fulfill their destiny. Rather, the *imago Dei* revealed the need to become *imago Christi* in order to realize their destiny as *gloria Dei*. True human likeness to God depends on the contradictory but harmonious process in which there is a simultaneous differentiation/identification of human beings with God. In other words, human beings participate in the process of deification, reaching their eschatological destiny by becoming similar to God in their perichoretic relations, while at the same time, there is growing ontological dissimilarity.

Becoming Human in Community

The characteristic (love of difference) relations of *agape* point to love's necessary transformation, or "flip," into an eschatological *philia* (love of the like) as "in history, the messianic becoming-human of the human being remains incomplete and uncompletable" (ibid.). As long as human beings are disconnected from God's complete indwelling, as is necessarily the case in *creatio originalis*, human beings can never become true humanity. This inability of human beings as different to reach their end highlights the dynamic nature of Moltmann's understanding of reality. From humanity's creation in a godforsaken space, there has been from the beginning the need for redemption. Humanity's task was impossible—even without human rebellion—from the start because its goal could only be reached by being in the full presence of God. Yet, this is exactly what the act of creating a different Other prevented. Differentiation precedes and makes possible unity. In the case of creation, differentiation meant disconnection because of the need for relational space between God and his different

Other. Humanity necessarily had to go through the trauma of being isolated from God, and thereby historically impotent, in order to reach its eschatological goal of fellowship with God. Reality, as long as it is not yet fully indwelt by God, must reflect its forsaken, isolated nature and face the constant threat of annihilating nothingness.

The lack inherent in *creatio originalis* explains why Moltmann calls the believer to live in contrast—actually contradiction—to present society. As part of the differentiating movement, society can only reflect its godforsakenness. The believer reflects the perichoretic community to a hopeless reality. The follower of Christ cannot expect reality in its forsakenness to reveal God's presence until the forsakenness is overcome by God's presence. Hence, in the given context of forsakenness, the norm for the follower of Jesus is to live sacrificially in contrast to fallen reality as a way of pointing to the promise of the future coming of God. The antithesis between the forsakenness of creation and the follower of Christ and its resultant tensions will remain ever evident until the promise is fulfilled, as "it is only the eschatological annihilation of death, the redemption of the body on a new earth and under a new heaven, which will consummate the 'becoming' process of human beings, thereby fulfilling their creaturely destiny" (*GC* 227). As we have seen, the destiny of *creatio originalis,* including humans, is a becoming one with God through *theosis* while at the same time becoming increasingly ontologically dissimilar.

Moltmann's understanding of the 'becoming' nature of humanity is further evidenced by his view on the *dominium terrae*. The promise given to human beings regarding dominion over creation is interpreted eschatologically. He argues, "under the conditions of history and in the circumstances of sin and death, the sovereignty of the crucified and risen Messiah Jesus is the only true *dominium terrae*" (ibid.). It is important to again note Moltmann's linking of the condition of history with sin and death. If we return to *TH*, we see that Moltmann remains consistent in his understanding of history: "The stage for what can be experienced, remembered and expected as 'history' is set and filled, revealed and fashioned, by promise" (*TH* 107). The promise of *creatio nova* plays a central role in looking at human history because of the separation and forsakenness of *creatio originalis*. The lack of creation and human history is both the realization of God's absence and the invitation for his indwelling. History awaits its completion within the divine life.

History for Moltmann is always contingent, in process, and provisional. The promise of *dominium terrae* points forward to its fulfillment by the Messiah. This need for fulfillment, the necessity of becoming, lies at the heart of Moltmann's thought. When human beings were created, they already were deficient and needed the completion that only an intimate fellowship with God could provide. The human being who participates fully in the divine life when God arrives from the future must be understood to be significantly different than the original human being as she becomes God's same Other. The human being of *creatio originalis* is forsaken, isolated, and threatened by the nothingness. At her core, she yearns to be more. In the *creatio nova* the human being is embraced and indwelt by the divine community. She becomes "God's glory in the world—*gloria Dei est homo*" (*GC* 228). There is no lack as she is ful/filled by God. The human being finds her true identity within the reciprocal, perichorectic, fail-safe exchanges of *philia*. In summary, Moltmann says, "we can say that as God's image human beings conform to the presence of the Creator in his creation, and as God's children they conform to the presence of God's grace; but when the glory of God itself enters creation, they will become like God and transfigured into his appearance" (ibid.). The image always directs beyond itself to the reality to which it corresponds. Conforming to Christ as the image of God is not enough, one must become like God: "The *imago per conformitatem gratiae* points beyond itself to the *imago per similitudinem gloriae*" (*GC* 229).

The human as becoming has two distinct meanings for Moltmann, in synch with two concurrent and distinct directions. In the direction of *creatio originalis*, history, and ordinary time, becoming is an ongoing movement of differentiation with the realization of forsakenness, futility, and the *nihil*. But in the countering movement of identification, *creatio nova* and *perichoresis*, becoming has an eschatological end in fulfillment; as humanity is drawn into the interpenetrating relationships of divine life. Humans, simultaneously, become unlike God as they eschatologically become like God.

The Ethics of Kenosis and *Theosis*

In making inner-trinitarian relationships the ideal for human relationality, Moltmann's ethics privileges the unity-in-diversity of *perichoresis*. Though *philia* transforms, or "flips," into *agape* for the sake of difference in the movement of history, *agape* again transmutes, or "re-flips" into *philia* for creation to be completed. The risk of kenosis is superceded and suspended by the safety of *theosis*. The perfect community is revealed as "the unselfishness in the eternal love and unity of the trinitarian God is *perichoresis*: community in mutual interdependence and interpenetration" (*UL* 119).

The focus on relationality leads Moltmann to conclude that "God is not subject, God is community" (UL 120).

However, even as God's different Other, community is also the goal of creation. The problem for creation is that as God's different Other, it finds itself in a place of abandonment and forsakenness by God. In the space threatened by death and annihilation, humanity lacks both the safety and wherewithal for perichoretic relations to exist. Forsaken creation is too inherently distant from God, and in its distance too vulnerable to rejection, and even violence. The only way to perichoretic community for creation is to experience the redemption of God through Christ in the power of the Spirit. Creation in its original forsakenness is raised up into the divine community by the God who becomes vulnerable to suffering through the incarnation of the Son. Once humanity experiences life in the divine community by God's saving act, it can attempt to live kenotically in the midst of forsakenness.

As God comes from the future, *theosis* is not a healing restoration, rather, *theosis* is the overcoming of creation's limit so it may participate in the divine *perichoresis*. And with that overcoming, although creation is validated as necessary to the process, the differentiations of creation are invalidated. Human beings are empowered to strive for *perichoresis* in forsakenness because of the model established by the sending of the Son. The sending of the Son to redeem creation reveals the kenotic nature of divine life as it becomes vulnerable to the different Other. God continues to give himself in spite of, and because of, the possibility of rejection. The gift of the Son opens the divine community to creation and reveals to creation the path it should follow. Like the Son, creation should exist kenotically for the different Other in spite of, and because of, the lack of assurance regarding the receptivity of the Other. Because God has not yet fulfilled his promise to dwell fully in creation, living kenotically for forsaken humanity means exposing oneself to the risk present in the face of the powers of evil and suffering. Jesus Christ is the example to follow in this context. Jesus Christ humbled himself to the point of bearing death on the cross. So also, in the midst of evil, the followers of Jesus Christ are to make themselves vulnerable to the violent by reacting non-violently for the sake of the violent Other.

Moltmann's understanding of an ethics of discipleship as kenosis is consistent with the ethical impulses that eschatological theology had from the very beginning. In *TH*, Moltmann emphasizes "the promised identity of man leads into the differentiation of self-emptying" (*TH* 91). He further explains "man does not gain himself by distinguishing himself from 'the world', but by emptying himself into it" (*TH* 92). Self-emptying was never to be seen as the end goal. Rather, it was part of the process of receiving his true self: "He gains himself by abandoning himself. He finds life by taking death upon him. He attains to freedom by accepting the form of a servant" (ibid.). Throughout his work on the crucified God and the development of a social doctrine of the Trinity, Moltmann's basic ethical stance has changed little. Moltmann summarizes this position when he says, "true love is the unselfish surrender to another person or other beings for their own sake. Reciprocal kenotic love sustains the world. It depletes the world 'in reference to inherent existence' while it enlivens the world through the realization of perichoretic community" (*UL* 121). This understanding of ethics as kenosis is possible because Moltmann understands kenosis as intertwined with *theosis* in a process that yields *perichoresis*, which is the very nature of God as Trinity.

Kenosis and *theosis* are identifiable as the two simultaneous, contradictory movements present in Moltmann's understanding of reality. As shown by the analogy of relationality, both kenosis and *theosis* exist at every level of reality. Whenever the movement of reality is towards differentiation, there is a kenosis that creates the possibility of re-establishing unity. Whenever the transposition is made through the unselfish giving of oneself to the Other and the movement is towards unity, *theosis* exists as the processing unity which is shaped through the reciprocating interpenetration and indwelling of one another. In kenosis, *agape* creates new possibilities out of difference. In *theosis*, *philia* love forms deeper and deeper connections in the context of (dis)similarity. As *perichoresis* develops, it concurrently validates and invalidates the differentiation that made kenosis necessary. Kenosis precedes and makes possible identification. This dialectic of kenosis and *theosis* is perfected at the ultimate level of reality within divine life. When God becomes "all in all," all of reality will be raised up into the divine perichoretic community. Here disconnection and forsakenness will be experienced no longer as God's presence fulfills his promise. From the future, God will come to complete himself and his creation.

Choosing to Be Guilty

As the exploration of the *theosis*/kenosis dialectic demonstrates for Moltmann, the ethical—the way of Jesus Christ—is the way of self-emptying and non-violence. *Imago Christi* requires, no questions asked, self-sacrifice. However, strikingly and paradoxically—even if understandably in light of the exigencies of daily life—after all the emphasis on living kenotically,

Moltmann allows for, moreover adapts, Bonhoeffer's responsible action which he describes as "the readiness to incur guilt" (*EH* 142).[20] Where non-violence encounters the violence of a power-over, the question of the legitimate use of power comes to the fore. Although Moltmann's basic ethical stance requires that the follower of Christ kenotically give herself to the violent Other in the hope of redemption, Moltmann recognizes that in some instances, the goal of liberation from violence can only be initiated through violent resistance. In other words, Moltmann asserts "the principle of non-violent action does not exclude the struggle for power" (*WJC* 130). Sometimes, according to Moltmann, there is a necessary "struggle for power," a struggle "to make every exercise of power subject to law" (ibid.). Moltmann simultaneously argues that resistance to illegitimate force is an understandable use of power and that violent acts of resistance are never justifiable. Forceful resistance to violence may be necessary and understandable at times for Moltmann in the Christian life. However to say violent acts were justifiable, in any instance, would be to deny the ideal of non-violent action. In personal conversation, Moltmann explained that he carried two principles from his participation in WWII. First, he would never pick up arms again. Second, he would never allow a tyrant like Hitler to maintain power again. In spite of the contradiction, Moltmann felt he had to hold onto the way of non-violence, but he would "choose to be guilty" if the situation demanded it.[21]

This position is consistent with Moltmann's assertions regarding Christian political participation. In the face of tyranny, "resistance is called for . . . in order to safeguard the rights of the neighbor and to protect the powerless" (*EH* 130). He makes an even stronger statement when he declares, "active resistance for the sake of the oppressed neighbor is not only a right but also a duty of the Christian" (*EH* 129). This violence "cannot be approved but can be answered for" (*EH* 143). In the violence of active resistance "guilt remains guilt, but we can live with this guilt" (ibid.). As *agape*, active resistance is "selfless to the point of sacrific[ing] personal innocence" (ibid.).

---

20. Bonhoeffer explains: "When a man takes guilt upon himself in responsibility, and no responsible man can avoid this, he imputes this guilt to himself and to no one else; he answers for it; he accepts responsibility for it. He does not do this in the insolent presumptuousness of his own power, but he does it in the knowledge that this liberty is forced upon him and that in this liberty he is dependent upon grace. Before other men the man of free responsibility is justified by necessity; before himself he is acquitted by his conscience, but before God he hopes only for mercy" (*Ethics*, 113).

21. Personal conversation with the author, Tübingen, January 1993.

Violent acts of resistance may be understandable, but they certainly do not coincide with the norm of *perichoresis*. Nevertheless, in the face of an all-consuming violent Other, one can (must?), according to Moltmann, legitimately resist.[22] In such cases for Moltmann, as Wiebe explains, it is "a matter of love being ready to incur guilt, for this is still violence that cannot be approved but that can be answered for."[23] At this point, according to Wiebe, "the issue for Moltmann is no longer one of violence or nonviolence, but of the criteria which may be used to govern the justifiable use or unjustifiable use of power."[24]

In a violent context, we can choose to be guilty by retaliating with violence; for example, to prevent further bloodshed of innocent lives. In retaliating, we may be justified in our actions and such actions are understandable; however, guilt is still suffered. Wiebe describes Moltmann's position as one that while giving preference to non-violence means we cannot begin with a "principle of non-violence" because we live in a world "where politics is a matter of power, distribution of power, and participation in the exercise of power."[25] However, stepping outside the norm of *perichoresis* in order to preserve ourselves results in the loss of hope for reconciliation between the self and the violent Other. Moltmann allows for a struggle in resistance.[26] But the struggle is not ultimately to replace one form of oppression with another. Just as "love of an enemy can never be subjection to the enemy" (*WJC* 130), the struggle for legitimate use of power can never climax in the subjection of the enemy.

Rather, in each instance, the intent is to create a climate in which there can be a free giving of oneself to the Other. For Moltmann, the norm for humanity is always the kenosis of Christ, for it is only in this way that trinitarian *perichoresis* can be imaged in the human community. Yet, because of Moltmann's knowledge of the millions of oppressed whom their oppressors have killed especially in this century, he allows for the possibility of a violent resistance. In such cases, violence is returned for violence and the followers of Christ willingly incur guilt for the protection of the weak. But God can "transform human guilt into divine suffering" as he "bears not only the history of (the world's) suffering but also the history of human injustice" (*HTG* 50).

22. See *EH* 129, 138.
23. Wiebe, "Revolution," 110.
24. Ibid.
25. Ibid.
26. See *EH* 129–38.

Questions and Ambiguities

As Moltmann develops *perichoresis* and an ethics of discipleship, the relationships between difference and sameness, kenosis and *theosis*, and *agape* and *philia* reveal a dynamic reality that has a comprehensive coherence and even exquisite profundity about it. However, it also raises important and puzzling questions.[27] The reality that Moltmann, in spite of his ethics of kenosis, allows for forceful resistance to violence is of crucial significance for our exploration. It means that his intention to provide unequivocal ethical leverage for daily living is not as unproblematic as it appears in first reading that "discipleship commits us to nonviolence."[28]

Self-sacrifice is, for Moltmann, clearly the normative ethical response. This would seem to mean that an *imitatio Christi* requires self-sacrifice in any case of violence. The complexity of a kenotic ethics is understood when Moltmann presents the two views of the self. In *creatio originalis*, self-assertion is a choosing to be guilty and a forsaking of the Other. In the perichoretic Trinity, self-assertion is natural, legitimate, and morally commendable. Since for Moltmann creation is both forsaken and indwelt, the question remains for human beings: when we act in self-assertion are we to consider ourselves "guilty" or "justified"?

Here we can sense the depth of the ethical dilemma in which Moltmann finds himself, and we with Moltmann. Being both conformed to God and becoming like God entail a ceaseless self-giving. With this giving comes the promise/reality of a divine indwelling in the openness of the self. However, "choosing to be guilty" fits with neither conforming to God nor being like God. Yet it is a choice intentionally embraced by Moltmann. What does this "inconsistency" tell us about the cash-value of Moltmann's ethical theory for the ethical conundrums of daily life? How does one know when to choose to be guilty?

---

27. These questions arise in spite of the recognition of Moltmann's influence on liberation theology, especially in the work of Boff and Sobrino. Thompson, in *Modern Trinitarian Perspectives*, 120ff., traces the influence of Moltmann's doctrine of the Trinity on social and political reality in liberation theologians in. The Marxist connection with liberation theology also relies upon a dynamic (Hegelian) understanding of reality, but it is not clear that key concepts like "God's preferential option for the poor" find more resonance in the life of the Trinity than the kingdom of God. It seems that oppression understood as sin against the trinitarian communion downplays the suffering of the human community. See also Phillips, *The Use of Scripture*.

28. Schuurman deduces, "Moltmann does offer some moral guidance toward a constructive social ethic, but I would argue that this positive guidance is not connected to or based upon his eschatology" ("Creation, Eschaton, and Ethics," 51).

In light of his understanding of self-assertion, is a choosing to be guilty ever a morally commendable position? It is certainly not clear. That being the case, we are left somewhat in the lurch as to which way to act. This ambiguity suggests the inability, or at least limited ability, of Moltmann's position for providing ethical help for people of faith.[29]

In fact, Moltmann's ambiguity at this point even suggests that his thought could be used to support a militaristic regime as well as asceticism or pacifism. What are the criteria that help us determine when we are justified to pick up arms and choose to be guilty? Or do we need to live with the reality that, although never justified, sometimes we find ourselves with the only resort of armed violence?

Another question becomes paramount in this discussion: Is the "end" (goal) of being human the termination of being human (*theosis*)?[30] Or is the end of being human accomplished in perichoretic communion? Or, as the thrust of our argument would suggest, are both true at the same time for Moltmann? In many ways, perhaps most, it may not make too much difference. But at least in a couple of ways, I suggest, matters of practical ethical significance are at stake. If essential to the difference that characterizes creation is godforsakenness and the suffering it entails, does not Moltmann come close (too close in my view) to constructing—his intentions notwithstanding—a theodicy which to a large degree ontologizes, and in that way, justifies suffering and evil as necessary and inevitable? This seems to amount to an eschatological justification of evil and suffering as they are transmuted, or "flipped," into a greater good.

Within the context of fallen creation, redeemed humanity becomes a contradiction of social order. Ethics are kenotic because the lack in *creatio originalis* does not allow the possibility of mutuality. Within the God-filled creation of the eschaton, humanity ceases to be a conforming image and becomes a partnering image in the divine community. As necessarily perichoretic, such relationships do not stand in need of ethical direction. As true as this may be when we are home with God in glory, in this fallen world, with its penultimate here and now, we still require ethical direction.

---

29. Wiebe poses the issue: "If the criterion is Christ, it cannot come out of a self-interpreting situation . . . all ideas that make a claim to have authority apart from or over against Christ must be tested and seen for what they are" ("Revolution," 120).

30. Here I draw upon Derrida's play with the meanings of end in "The Ends of Man." It seems that for Moltmann the eschatological end of humanity stands in contrast to its creational end.

Human beings, which start out as God's (dis)similar Other in his original act of creation, become God's (dis)similar Other in the fulfillment of the promise. As it is raised into the divine community, humanity moves from the realm of difference and freedom to the realm of sameness and necessity. Moltmann argues that "the eschatological becoming-one-with God of human beings is inherent in the concept of 'seeing', for the seeing face to face and the seeing him as he is transforms the seer into the One seen and allows him to participate in the divine life and beauty" (*GC* 229). The ultimate effects of "participation in the divine nature and conformity to God, flowering into perfect resemblance, are the marks of the promised glorification of human beings" (ibid.). The complication here is that "glorification" ironically has both the connotation of the suspension of being human and the surpassing of being human.

With this construction come some very real pastoral questions: When God's suffering is conceived of in this way, is God's suffering, in the final analysis, real suffering? It seems to have a fail-safe quality to it because redemption and glorification are already built into creation's story by God from the beginning.[31] The Hell of suffering becomes only a temporary, but inherent, way-station to *theosis*.

A related concern has to do with the very real difference regarding the risk taken by God and the risk inherent to human life. In the kenotic actions of the Son, the kenotic way of being human is revealed. Kenosis implies risk and, for Moltmann, there exists analogy between human and divine risk. This analogy is possible because God takes human suffering into himself. The tension here between divine power and divine love is most radically felt. God's glory is understood as his ability to be vulnerable rather than in his infinite strength. But if God being almighty is linked with his vulnerability, his "almightiness" is limited because God's exposure to risk is limited. The risk God takes in experiencing suffering is, I would argue, not truly a risk, because the God coming from the future always has enough power to overcome suffering and death. It is true that in Moltmann's understanding of divine love, God is selfless and "risks" himself for the sake of the suffering Other. Yet, that risk is wholly relativized by the fact that the kenotic movement of God is simultaneously, from the beginning, always countered by a *theosis* in which God is once again

---

31. McDougall argues correctly that Moltmann's understanding of friendship involves self-giving love (*Pilgrimage of Love*, 144ff.). She assumes this means *agape* for Moltmann. I understand both *agape* and *philia* to be self-giving love; the difference is context. Because of the predictable responses involved in the self-giving of *philia* there is little risk. The analogy between divine life and human community is harder to establish given this difference.

"all in all." The limitation of the divine risk is noted by Jüngel, when he points out, quoting Barth, that "God gives himself, but does not give himself away."[32] God is never totally at risk in his self-gift because of the assured divine delimitation. *Theosis* always accompanies kenosis.[33] However, for creatures the risk is never fail-safe. Oppressed people face real risk and can only hope for freedom from suffering through the actions of the divine Other. Their risk of suffering is more ambiguous, without built-in guarantees. However, in Moltmann's theory, God's sacrificial suffering is simultaneously countered by God's redemptive action.

The quandaries of Moltmann's ethics, at this point, are many. However, they seem to follow from the fact that he begins with a creation that is not good, but forsaken. When one begins here—in spite of all subsequent compensatory moves—human inadequacies, ugliness and even sin become watermarks of humanity, not by the contingency of disobedience, but by the necessity of creation, even as concurrently, redemption from suffering and perichoretic community is the end of being human.

---

32. Jüngel, *The Doctrine of the Trinity*, 84.

33. Highfield, in "Divine Self-Limitation," rejects Moltmann's theology of divine self-limitation because a conception of a God who must limit himself to create and save "suffers under the prior limit of that very necessity" (68).

CHAPTER 7

The Ethics of Ambiguity

Self-Sacrifice and Self-Assertion

Moltmann's understanding of difference, as we have seen, is ultimately rooted in a cosmogony that views reality in terms of fundamental contradictory oppositions.[1] Reality in its differentiation is driven towards its fulfillment by the tension between two simultaneous, opposing movements.[2] Difference and unity are accounted for in terms of these contradictory movements. In the end, the tension between his final all-inclusive and cosmically contradictory assertions that "God will be all in all" and "greater ontological differences" continues unresolved.[3] Nevertheless, and simultaneously, in the eschatological direction, in the harmonic feast of Sabbath Redemption, kenosis transmutes into theosis in what could be called the triumph of glory.

In this final chapter we will examine some of the implications of his cosmogony for ethical direction in the push and pull of ordinary life. A

---

1. Interestingly, Gunton suggests that many of Moltmann's much criticized tendencies may be a result of "too great a preoccupation with apologetic questions" (*The Promise of Trinitarian Theology*, 23). The tie between apologetics and metaphysics is evident in the history of Christian theology and philosophy. Moltmann's appeal to a contradictory/harmonic monism can, I think, be seen as an apologetic move. While there may indeed be apologetic value, my point is that such a move may have unintended consequences. Dalferth sees trinitarian thought as an attempt to move beyond Enlightenment theism and atheism and move beyond the modern speculative tradition. But I have argued that Moltmann's thought is not a move beyond speculative thought, but has moved from the binary opposition of the Enlightenment by appealing to an ontology which reconciles opposites.

2. For an account of Thomas' understanding of difference as preceding opposition, see Cunningham, *Genealogy of Nihilism*, 219ff.

3. Milbank argues that "the very perfection of relation between Father and Son is in danger of obliterating the usual significance of personal relatedness" ("The Second Difference," 230).

cluster of questions that have surfaced in our earlier discussions will serve as the backdrop for our considerations:

1. In view of Moltmann's *zimzum* theory of creation as God-forsaken, is it possible for Moltmann to fully affirm the original goodness and worth of creation? Or does Moltmann's cosmogony which, in and through its validation of finite diversity and differentiation, prioritizes infinite unity, cast too long a shadow over finite creational diversity and creaturely distinctiveness?[4]

2. Does the inherent deficiency of created reality as godforsaken, which necessitates from the beginning redemptive fulfilling, entail that Moltmann is unable to do full justice to both the radical nature of sin and evil as the irresponsible turning away from God and God's ways of love, as well as to the unmerited, gracious redemption through the death and resurrection of Jesus Christ? So despite Moltmann's assertion that evil is contingent and non-necessary, when "the cross is at the centre of the Trinity . . . Before the world was, the sacrifice was already in God. No Trinity is conceivable without the Lamb, without the sacrifice of love, without the crucified Son" (*TK* 83), is it not also implied that, when all is said and done, sin and evil and concomitant suffering come with the creation as a necessary part of the cosmic fabric?[5]

All of these questions find their resonance in the focal concern of this chapter. Does Moltmann's cosmogony lead, as he intends, to a practical theology with ethical guidance for daily living? One sizeable obstacle, which makes answering this question extremely difficult, is the fact that Moltmann's ethics too often remains at the level of general principles and abstraction. Furthermore, even though his call to the self-sacrifice of kenosis is constant and impassioned, his recognition that sometimes (often? seldom? usually?) we need to be self-assertive and "choose to be guilty" seriously muddies the ethical waters.[6]

---

4. Levinas, in "Ethics of the Infinite," critiques any eschatology that fuses. He explains, "I am trying to work against this identification of the divine with unification or totality. Man's relationship with the other is *better* as difference than as unity: sociality is better than fusion" (74). While Moltmann also wants to stress sociality, divine and creational, his eschatological focus suggests fusion.

5. Jansen asks, in his analysis of Moltmann's position on suffering: "Must God not suffer, whether he wills it or not? The concept of active suffering (God choosing to suffer) appears to remain a matter of choice rather than of necessity" (*Relationality*, 134).

6. Compare with Milbank's argument in "Can Morality be Christian?" that a characteristic of Christianity is "the end of sacrifice." See also Edith Wyschogrod, *Saints and Postmodernism*, 95ff., on saints and the renunciation of power.

In the push and pull of daily life, it is my suspicion that Moltmann often leaves us ill at ease; ethically in the lurch, usually with heightened feelings of guilt for so often finding it impossible to walk the royal road of kenotic self-sacrifice.[7] Is the need and reality of "choosing to be guilty" in Moltmann's thought the exception which proves the rule, or is this need for self-assertion built-in to his cosmogony as the dialectically oppositional complement to the call to constant self-surrender? In any case, Moltmann's call to ethical kenosis is not without attendant ambiguities.[8]

If the exception is, in fact, the route most people find themselves on in the hurly-burly of life, doesn't that cast a considerable shadow over the viability and credibility of his kenotic ethics, or at least make it an idealistic ethics that remains out of reach most of the time for all but the most saintly among us? On the other hand, if in fact self-assertion is recognized as a necessary, if not laudable part of creational life, how can we avoid the conclusion that Moltmann's ethics is, in effect and reality, an ethics of considerable ambiguity for people in the throes of life?

Creation as "the Tragedy of Divine Love"

Moltmann, as I have repeatedly underscored, begins by defining God's act of creating as an act in which God suffers a self-limitation. Consequently, "the temporality of earthly creation does not reflect the presence of God—it reflects his absence" (*COG* 284). This dictates that from the very beginning, "in the *primordial moment* . . . before the creation of the world" (*COG* 282), whatever else shows up in history, "the deliverance or redemption of the world is bound up with the self-deliverance of God from his sufferings" (*TK* 60).

Here, I suggest—despite all the virtues and breakthroughs which Moltmann's theology incarnates—is the heart of the problem which specter-like haunts Moltmann's thought at every turn.

---

7. Again, Moltmann has inspired much reflection on many of these issues. One only need look at the essays by Volf, Sobrino, and Cone in *The Future of Theology*, written in honor of Moltmann, to see the work his thought has invited.

8. Dalferth understands the doctrine of the Trinity to suggest an ontology which "is not a desriptive conceptual account of divine activity as such. It is an attempt to spell out the conditions and presuppositions without which the eschatological experience of the risen Christ could not be true" ("The Eschatological Roots of the Doctrine of the Trinity," 168). Furthermore, he suggests that "the doctrine of the Trinity does not offer a concept of God but insists on the fundamental and irrevocable difference between God and all our models . . ." (ibid., 169). He seems to be pointing to the difference between confessing God as Trinity in faith and conceptually grasping the inner life of God. It is my contention that Moltmann blurs this distinction. See also Ingolf Dalferth, *Existenz Gottes*.

The history of creation is for Moltmann to be seen as "the tragedy of divine love" (*TK* 59), because "for God, creation means self-limitation, the withdrawal of himself, that is to say self-humiliation" (ibid.). And even though Moltmann also insists with equal passion that "creation is part of the eternal love affair between God the Father and God the Son" (ibid.), temporal creation never overcomes its initial handicap of being God-forsaken. With creation God's self-humiliation begins; "the self-limitation of the One who is omnipresent, and the suffering of eternal love" (ibid.).

Instead of positively affirming in faith that God as love calls creation into being, and since God is God, the realities of space-limitation (space only being a mode of creational existence) do not hold for God, Moltmann insists that "the creator has to concede to his creation the space in which it can exist." Indeed, "if God were omnipresent in the absolute sense, and manifested his glory, there would be no earthly creation. In order to make himself endurable for his earthly creatures, God has to veil his glory . . . Remoteness from God and spatial distance from God result from the withdrawal" (*COG* 306) of God. Analogously, "God [primordially] restricts his eternity so that in this primordial time he can give his creation time. God becomes the "space" of the world and gives creation "time.""

Consequently, "creative love is always a suffering love as well," (*TH* 59) and the fundamental dynamics of Moltmann's cosmogony are set in place. Withdrawal, remoteness, and forsakenness cannot be the last words. Derestriction, intimate indwelling, manifestation of glory, and redemption are equiprimordial co-simultaneous movements.

Not only is God the space of the world, but also the world is God's space," the *spacial* creation will then become an omnipresent creation" (*COG* 294). Not only is earthly time "the time of transience . . . a form of life into the form of death" (*COG* 283), and "the time of history" "exile, as the far country and remoteness of God" (*COG* 304), but "the *temporal* creation will then become an eternal creation, because all things will participate in God's eternity" (*COG* 294). The history of creation as the "tragedy of divine love" is transformed and overturned into the history of redemption and "the feast of eternal joy" (*TK* 59).

Instead of creation as a with-space, a space for moving with God, from the outset, creation is an opposed-space, a space of "detachment from God" and for "freedom of movement over against God" (*COG* 306).[9] Creation, it would appear, is as much original curse as original blessing. Indeed, Moltmann talks of "the first temporal and imperfect creation"

---

9. See Volf, "Creation, Eschaton, and Social Ethics."

(*COG* 91), a "creation aligned towards its redemption from the very beginning" (*COG* 264).

The very existence of creation as creation is already a demerit, an absence, a distance from God, a distance that "needs" redemption. The original separation from God—without any human intent or misdeed—is already conceived as an oppositional "movement against God." No wonder that, in terms of God's primordial self-limitation, Moltmann talks of a hell in the primordial *nihil,* making, so to speak, a space for evil which precedes the fall. Separation from God is a cosmic fault-line running through creation, and sin and evil are accidents waiting to happen, only a matter of time, of "*Chronos,*" as "the power of futility" (*COG* 284) before they erupt (*COG* 306). The result is that a "frailty of the temporal creation of human beings is like a detonator for the sin of wanting to be equal to God and to overcome this frailty" (*COG* 91). Much later in the same book Moltmann summarizes: "If God himself enters into his creation through his Christ and his Spirit . . . he will then overcome not only the God-forsakenness of sinners, but also the distance and space of his creation itself, which resulted in isolation from God, and sin" (*COG* 306). Again this would seem to make the fall into sin more of a function of creational finitude than human irresponsibility. In *Experiences of God* he writes that "the enslavement under which the created being suffers is transience" (111).

Indeed, when in *GC* Moltmann speaks of the *coelum naturae,* or heaven of nature, which contains alongside of "constructive potentialities" that have "ontological priority before the kingdom of the world's reality" (*GC* 166) certain "potencies which do not belong to the human sphere but which yet have a destructive effect on that sphere" (*GC* 169), it is difficult to avoid wondering if evil is not in some way being woven into the fabric of creation.

God and Suffering

For Moltmann, God's creative love is inherently a suffering love. Indeed, "God and suffering belong together" (*TK* 49). For him, "the suffering of God with the world, the suffering of God from the world, and the suffering of God for the world are the highest forms of his creative love" (*TK* 60).

I regard Moltmann's emphasis on God's suffering as most welcome in contrast to the traditions that do not accept the passion of God. A loving God, it would seem clear, would suffer with his creation. However, for Moltmann, God does not just suffer on account of sin and evil. Instead

God's suffering begins in the act of creating, which Moltmann conceives as a humiliating self-limitation.

This seems most problematic and, in my view, skews the entire subsequent discussion of God's suffering with and from creation. I see no reason to consider the original loving act of creation as a self-limitation that causes God to suffer. Rather, God took delight in pouring out his love creatively, declaring that it was good, and walking with Adam and Eve in the cool of the day in the garden of this earth called Eden. In the overflow of creative love, God took a "beautiful risk" and was vulnerable.

Only when, in the mystery of sin and evil, humankind turned their backs on God and on each other, did God's vulnerable risk turn into suffering.[10] God's suffering, then, is a suffering with and from a creation entangled in evil. As love, God could only reach out and keep coming again and again, calling humankind and creation back to the ways of love and justice, and in the death and resurrection of Jesus Christ show that love is stronger than death.

In other words, since for Moltmann creation is already a separating from God in which God "suffers," Moltmann sees no other way then to place the cross and suffering constitutively in the heart of the Trinity. This, among other things, leads him to contrast *agape,* the creative and suffering love of God for the other (and the like in the other), with *philia,* the engendering love of intra-trinitarian love of the like for the like (and for the other in the like).

All these moves and the distinctions they entail seem not only speculative, but would be unnecessary except for the fact that Moltmann begins with creation as self-restriction. Moltmann intends to develop a theory which does justice to the cross and resurrection. I am suggesting, however, that Moltmann's *zimzum* theory of creation not only fundamentally denigrates creaturely history, reality and time, but, by making the act of creating itself a negative separation from God, makes it highly difficult, if not impossible, for him to do sufficient justice to both the radical separation from God that is at the heart of sin and the gracious, unmerited redemption of the world in Jesus Christ.

In other words: when Moltmann places the cross and resurrection of Jesus Christ in the heart of God from the beginning, it would seem highly improbable, if not impossible, for Moltmann—no matter what the intention, no matter what the moves—to avoid leaving the impression that creation, and creational time and transience, are from the outset in

---

10. Walsh states succinctly, "Moltmann's view of creation . . . does not sufficiently account for the fall" ("Theology of Hope," 67).

some way impaired, and, even without the reality of sin and evil, need to be superseded and transformed. It further raises the question whether the built-in impairment of being human does not make actual sin and evil only a matter of time, in effect making humankind more victims of sin and evil than responsible agents of sin and evil. Separation from God that comes with being human, and separation from God which is sin, become inextricably entangled.

Moreover, if "God and suffering belong together" not due to the reality of sin and evil, but because the separation involved in creating (even if it is in love) is in the nature of God, does not this in a fundamental way make human suffering as separation and isolation from God an inevitable part of the cosmic machinery that is to be endured, in the hope of its relief in the coming redemption? Suffering as separation from God because of our creaturely condition would seem in some way to "normalize"—it's just part of created human nature—suffering, and take away from its incongruity, gratuitousness, unjustness, and horribleness.

Although Moltmann, undoubtedly, personally and existentially recognizes how terrible human suffering is, the fact that in his theory suffering comes with being human as a built-in, inescapable feature of creation from the beginning—a necessary, inescapable phase even without sin and evil along the road to the ultimate glory of redemption—nevertheless serves to mitigate or anesthetize the sting of suffering.

In Moltmann's cosmogony it appears to be the case that suffering and evil are themselves redeemed, not, as I would suggest is more in line with the biblical witness, that we are redeemed from suffering and evil.

Placing the cross in the heart of the Trinity would also seem to downplay the seriousness of sin as humankind turning away from God and rejecting the way of love. After all, "in the cross of Christ God took evil, sin and rejection on himself, and in the sacrifice of his infinite love transformed it into goodness, grace and election" (*SL* 212). According to Moltmann, God "moulds and alchemizes the pain of his love into atonement for the sinner" (*SL* 136). Evils too are transformed into good, and sins are redeemed. Questions multiply.

Does this do full justice to the reality of evil and its destructiveness? Does Moltmann in his vision of final all-embracing redemption not come close to finally defusing the radical antithesis between goodness and evil (even as he affirms it)?

By God's "primordial self-restriction" (*COG* 333), God created a space in which creation can be different. In this forsaken, free space, creation's response to God's loving overtures was not guaranteed. In the agapic love for that which is unlike, there is the possibility of God's offer of himself being rejected by creation. In this inter-mural relationship with a different Other, God is vulnerable, and suffers. God's very being as kenotic love seems to be at risk as creation refuses the gift. In this movement, an element of contingency, unpredictability, and risk is involved as creation refuses the gift.

At the same time, the structure of Moltmann's cosmogony insists that God's agapic kenosis for creation is superseded/surpassed by a theosis of creation. Because the God-forsaken space is in God, God can and does de-restrict himself and refill the space. The risk turns out, eschatologically, not to be a genuine risk. The central promise highlighted by the eschatological movement is that God will refill the forsaken space, thereby transforming temporal creation into the "eternal creation" (*COG* 295).

In the divine *perichoresis* with its mutual indwelling, there is a constant openness to the Other in the continual giving of the self. Since, however, this is the giving/receiving of the same Other characteristic of *philia*, this is an intramural, rather than inter-mural, relationship that is relatively predictable, even 'safe.' A loving response can always be expected from the Others who are essentially one and the same—like for like. While there are the distinct persons of Father, Son, and Spirit, their differentiation always/already presupposes a deeper unity that grounds the divine community. It is a loving of the Other in the like. Within the Trinity, any self-emptying through a self-gift is immediately responded to by a refilling self-gift by a (dis)similar Other in the dynamic nature of *perichoresis*. There is a constant overflowing from one into an Other. The cycle of giving and receiving is perpetual, but it is within a self-same threesome!

Once more, the same cluster of problems we have been working with in this chapter surface. The fact that promised redemption is not only expected, but necessary from the beginning, as well as the fact that theosis results in an "overriding harmony of the relations and of the self-transcending movements" (*CG* 103), would seem to call into question or lessen, if not nullify, the risk God assumes in creating the world. From the very beginning, it seems, this different Other has existed for the sake of God and for the sake of redemption. From the moment of its differentiation, creation has been on a journey of (re)identification and (re)unification with God through God's interpenetration and divinization of his different Other.

While creation's rejection of God is without doubt real and poignant for Moltmann, it is not only the contingent, freely chosen rejection of and estrangement from God, but also, simultaneously, a necessary penultimate stage in a process where God fulfills himself. In God's case the risk of agapic love is superseded by the inevitability of *philia* love.

This construction, I suggest, is not without its problems. If the *philia* love of God ensures the eventual return to God, God would seem to be finally immune from the risk of agapic love. Doesn't this in effect take the heart out of the risk, turning it into a necessary but temporary storm on the road to the glory of eternity? Is this true to the biblical picture of God ruing the day he created, grieving at the mess? Doesn't it skew the very nature of love as vulnerability and risk to insist that, already from before the beginning, the glory of the feast of redemption is a sure thing?

It is one thing, in faith, to live in the certainty of the resurrection and the triumph of love. It is another thing to translate that certainty into a theoretic conceptualization which seems to eclipse the risk and drama of human time and history, embracing it and transforming it finally into the fail-safe eternity of God's drama. No matter the qualifications—and Moltmann's contradictory harmony monism always has built-in qualifications—when the suffering, sin, and violence of human life is in any way made a necessary part of the cosmic drama which in the end will be embraced and transformed in redemption, Moltmann, in my view, is erecting a kind of eschatological verification theodicy.

If before the creation it is already in the cards that God's suffering and concomitant creational suffering is but a penultimate stage in the process of redemption, doesn't this serve, as we have noted already, to minimize the existential horror of human suffering by validating it, even as ultimately invalidating it? Suffering itself would seem to be eschatologically justified and redeemed. I would suggest, rather, that suffering is that from which we are to be redeemed, even as we are redeemed from sin and evil.

Difference as Opposition

In finally priortizing unity and harmony, Moltmann's contradictory/harmonic monism thematizes differentiation as a necessary but penultimate stage. In reality's movement, differentiation is a moving from the unity, but this movement-from is also reality's drive towards its goal of greater unity. Consequently, difference cannot be fully affirmed as good, but is considered a kind of evil necessary to reality's movement from unity to greater unity—what Milbank calls "necessary alienation."[11] Moltmann's cosmogony emplants alienation inherently into the narrative of reality. As a result, the radical nature of evil and the uselessness of suffering are

---

11. Milbank, "The Second Difference," 223.

ultimately relativized because this alienation is not the result of sinful disconnection from God, but is an inherent part of the cosmic machinery necessary for the process.[12] Without this tension of opposites, reality stagnates. Differentiation, as alienation from the unity, exists for the sake of greater eschatological unity. As reality reaches its goal of greater unity, alienation, suffering, and disconnection cease as oppositional boundaries are somehow transformed, or flipped, into a new unity.

As we have seen, particularly in the discussion regarding the act of creation, God stands in contradiction to any different Other. Even if Moltmann's refined distinctions found in *creatio originalis* and *creatio nova* are honored, the difference of creation is still viewed as a detachment from God, an opposition, and in that sense, a deficiency. However, when this lack is overcome in redemption, it would seem that genuine difference is, if not threatened, certainly eclipsed. As (dis)similar in *perichoresis*, creation may not become the Son, but Moltmann does argue that it becomes a son. Becoming a son means dwelling in the divine community, as "the God-likeness that belongs to creation in the beginning becomes the God-sonship and daughterhood in the messianic fellowship with the Son" (*GC* 229). This promised glorification of the Other leads to "participation in the divine nature and conformity to God, flowering into perfect resemblance" (ibid.). Participation and perfect resemblance imply a kind of fusion, if not confusion, of identity and a transmogrification of boundaries.

The Trinity as Social Program

Since, for Moltmann, creation in its forsakenness from the beginning awaits its redemption, he needs to find a place other than in creation to ground his ethics. So the Trinity becomes his social program and he locates the norm for human ethical life in divine relationality. For Moltmann the ultimate assurance of both creation's existence and creation's return to God was the sending of the Son. In the incarnation, the Son, as both creator and redeemer, becomes a different Other so that the Father can love in a context of difference. Jesus Christ becomes different by a "whole and genuine emptying of his divine form and his divinity as well as his divine power" (UL 119). It is "through the Son the divine Trinity throws itself open for human beings" (*GC* 243). This trinitarian openness in redemption means that, in Jesus Christ, God is "there *for us* in our guilt, to free us from its burden" ("The Passion of Christ," 22). The trinitarian community reveals

---

12. Milbank concludes that Moltmann's "tragic theology" embraces "a Hegelian theodicy in which necessary estrangement is justified by the final outcome" (ibid., 224).

itself to be "open" and "inviting," and at the same time all-embracing. The incarnation of Christ opens creation to an entirely different and contradictory direction, even as it reveals the way to eschatological union.

In Christ, God is not only the revealer, but also the revealed. While the community of inner-trinitarian life is revealed to be the destiny of forsaken creation, in the Son, inner-trinitarian life is also revealed to be the ethical norm for human relationships within the forsakenness. The Trinity is to become the social program for humanity.

Divine love, *agape,* in the incarnation direction of differentiation is kenotic. Likewise, the ethical ideal revealed by the incarnate Son for forsaken creation is kenosis. The self-gift is to be a withdrawal of self for the sake of the Other. In self-emptying, the self is opened to the Other with the hope for reciprocation: "The promised identity of man leads into the differentiation of self-emptying" (*TH* 91). Then again: "Man does not gain himself by distinguishing himself from 'the world,' but by emptying himself into it" (*TH* 92). To have the hope of the future one must follow Christ which "involves a practical discipleship that follows the messianic path his own life took; and that means an ethic which has to be made identifiably Christian" (*WJC* 118). The pain or suffering that result from this act is transcended by the assurance that it is a necessary part of the process of redemptive theosis whereby everyone is reconciled to each Other and to God.

Kenosis and the Exercise of Agape in the Face of Violence

In this emphasis on kenosis as the way to theosis and participation in the divine community, Moltmann aligns the way of creation with the way of Christ. God has revealed that faithfulness must remain kenotic even in the face of rejection. Following Christ means that in our context of isolation and violence we too must exercise creative *agape*.

However, the presence of a violent Other deeply challenges Moltmann's hope of making inner-trinitarian life the norm for humanity. Here Schuurman's analysis is apt: "this way of rooting the necessity of the incarnation in the divine nature as love is a good example of Gustafson's criticism that Moltmann's theology is anthropocentric. God cannot be God without man. The idea of God suffering eternally is also hard to grasp and support."[13] What direction does trinitarian life give forsaken humanity beyond giving ourselves over to the redemptive process? When confronted with violence, the ideal of community can be held up and we can be urged

13. Schuurman, "Creation, Eschaton, and Ethics," 62.

to give ourselves lovingly, but unlike the divine life we have neither the knowledge of the Other's response nor the power to redeem (overcome) the Other. As we have noticed, in God's case, the risk of agapic love is accompanied and finally superseded by the inevitability of *philia* love. How is this to work for humans? On the one hand, since the suffering and violence, however contingent, are inevitably taken up and redeemed in the feast of eschatological redemption, humans are called to bear the sacrifices of ethical self-surrender in hope of the coming redemption. On the other hand, since suffering and violence need to be resisted as implicated in the dynamics of sin, humans are allowed to fight back, defend themselves, and "choose to be guilty."

How are we to square Moltmann's allowing for a returning of violence in an act of self-protection with his impassioned call to self-kenosis? Does this point to a fundamental inconsistency in his ethics, or, as we suspect, is this blatant contradiction simply part and parcel of the contradictory nature of Moltmann's cosmogony.[14]

As we have explored, in Moltmann's contradictory/harmonic monism we find a consistent and final eschatological privileging of identity and unity at the expense of ontological difference and non-union in his "overriding harmony" (*GC* 103). Despite his insistence and desire to reconcile difference and unity, freedom and necessity, *agape* and *philia*, creation and new creation, and kenosis and theosis, in his thought the validation of the first term in each opposing pair takes place by means of its simultaneous invalidation by and transcendence of the second term.

The end goal of a greater community between God and creation overrides/supersedes and, in effect, calls into question the full creaturely goodness of creational diversity. The penchant for being taken up in the divine community in Moltmann's cosmogony means that ultimately the space of *creatio originalis* is for the purposes of being filled and superseded. The question re-emerges: Does this conceptualization do sufficient justice to finite time, creaturely difference, and creational goodness, or does creation suffer an eclipse in the final redemption?

What does seem clear is that creation as god-forsaken is never really a credible threat to God. God's suffering of self-restriction is at the same time, always and already a process of de-restriction and redemption. Ironically, in Moltmann's thought, the real risk for creation is not isolation and forsakenness in the alienation of sin, but the danger that creation loses

---

14. McDougall concludes that Moltmann's idea of the social trinitarian program does not "legislate a particular course of action in any given situation," but shows a theological cohesion between divine life and concrete practices of believers (*Pilgrimage of Love*, 147).

its finite identity, transience, and particularity in the over-riding drama of redemption.

Perichoresis and Gender Relations

One area where viewing difference as opposition and as a threat to diversity is obviously a cause for concern is in understanding gender relationships. As we have seen, (dis)similarity to God is found in human community. In the analogy between divine life and human life, there is "found in the differentiation in relationship, and the wealth of relationship in the differentiation" (*GC* 223).[15] This differentiation in relationship "constitutes the eternal life of the Father, the Son, and the Spirit, and among human beings determines the temporal life of women and men, parents and children" (ibid.). In both creational and divine relations differentiation simultaneously accompanies the movement of identification and unity. The Son and Spirit had to be differentiated from the Father in order for the eternal, perichoretic divine relationships to exist. Yet, the fellowship experienced in these relationships is constantly overcoming the original differentiation to achieve a new, deeper divine unity. Creation had to be differentiated from God in order for it to exist in relationship with God as his different Other. Yet, through God's giving of himself to creation, creation is fulfilled and experiences God's indwelling and interpenetration. This is the ideal for all human relationality, as the "socially open companionship between people is the form of life which corresponds to God" (*GC* 223). The result is that "the trinitarian concept of community is able to overcome, not merely the ego-solitariness of the narcissist, but also the egoism of the couple" (ibid.).[16]

Moltmann also appeals to the Trinity to understand the relationship between "being sexually differentiated and sharing a common humanity" (*GC* 222). Through the revelation of the perichoretic community the similarity to God can be seen in "the sexual differentiation and community of human beings" (ibid.). The analogy of relationality establishes the connection between God and humanity. The community of humans is evident as "from the very outset human beings are social beings. They are aligned towards human society and are essentially in need of help" (*GC* 223). But the sexual similarity is not as evident. The question quickly becomes:

---

15. Sponheim, in *Faith and the Other*, 47ff., questions whether Moltmann's appeal to the analogy of relation works against an understanding of humanity as fully embodied.

16. And, as evidenced by his previous critique in *TK* of hierarchical understandings of human institutions, Moltmann maintains that the trinitarian concept of community can also overcome the oppression present in the state and the church.

"what is the nature of the God who in his image appears in male and female form?" (ibid.). He must turn to this question about humanity because he cannot begin with an assertion about humanity and project it upon God. As image, humanity can only be understood as indirect knowledge of God and not the grounds for an analogy.

Sexual differentiation and human community do point to an acknowledgment that the similarity to God "can be lived only in human community." (*GC* 222) However, in retrospect, the similarity is recognized only inasmuch as the human community participates in trinitarian *perichoresis*.[17] Trinitarian differentiation functions as a norm for human sexuality and cannot reflect a projection of human sexual difference upon God. The model for living in community must come from God's direct self-revelation. The best way to describe the nature of "God who in his image appears in male and female form" is according to Moltmann "the later doctrine of the Trinity, which discovers in God difference and unity . . . so that it talks about the God who is in his very self community and a wealth of different relationships" (*GC* 223). The analogy presented by Moltmann understands that a similar play between the movements of differentiation and unity can be found in human relationality. The differentiation between sexes is a prime example for Moltmann as "sexual difference . . . belongs to the very image of God itself" (*GC* 222). In human sexual relationships difference precedes and makes possible intimate relationships. Cunningham explains that "the relational differences of the Three [describe] them all as not merely *equal to*, but ultimately indistinguishable from *one another*."[18] In such relationships, the fellowship overcomes the isolation as community forms. In the sexual relationship, there is no hierarchical lording over, but a complete giving and receiving of the Other. This complete giving and receiving constantly calls forth new levels of intimacy. This pattern of differentiation preceding and making possible a complete giving and receiving is not limited to the human sexual relationship. Humanity's understanding of true community comes from its knowledge of the perichoretic trinitarian relationships.

But has Moltmann really given us a model that honors gender difference? *Perichoresis*, as we have seen, does involve (dis)similarity, but it is a dissimilarity among those with a shared essence.[19] The perichoretic community

17. Volf, in *Exclusion and Embrace*, 167ff., gives his account of gender identity rooted in trinitarian thought, which includes a summary discussion of the critique and response offered by feminist thought.

18. Cunningham, *These Three are One*, 43.

19. Rogers, in *Sexuality and the Christian Body*, addresses the complicated issues surrounding sexual identity and divine life for trinitarian theology.

may contain "a wealth of relations," but, in the end, it is about otherness in likeness. This may be fitting in reference to the Trinity. But does it do justice to the difference and diversity of human relationships, for example; man-woman, parent-child, teacher-student, government-citizens? Divine community may suggest the normativity of non-hierarchical relationships characterized by reciprocity. However, without holding to a basic sense of difference between those in relation, creational differences are bracketed, if not obliterated. By attempting to ground gender relations in some type of divine universal relationship, it seems difficult for Moltmann to avoid the charge of Irigaray that in such cases God "guarantees the social order that corresponds to a particular era."[20] LaCugna makes a similar point in her critique of some feminist theologies.[21] By appealing to God's relational life "it seems that feminism, as much as patriarchy, projects its vision of what it wishes would happen in the human sphere onto God, or onto a transeconomic, transexperiential realm of intradivine relations."[22]

Both Irigaray's and LaCugna's cautions flow from a concern that neither the experience of creational difference be read upon the divine community nor divine similarity be read into human community. How does this relate to what is above it? Certainly Moltmann would argue that he is doing neither.[23] But in making the (dis)similarity of participants in the divine community as normative for human relations, I would argue, he does not take seriously the firm boundaries of creational dissimilarities, gender differences being only one example.[24]

20. Irigaray, *I Love to You*, 44. As she states, "between man and woman, there really is otherness." Where Moltmann suggests a common humanity shared by the genders, an implication of Irigaray's view of difference is the rejection of the "illusion of the reduction to identity" (ibid., 61). Rather than the identity or unity found in Moltmann's view of differentiation, Irigaray wants to speak of recognition, of companions, and of "the transfiguration of desire *for* the other (as an object?) into a desire *with* the other" (ibid., 139). Moltmann has inspired and interacted with feminist theology; for example, see Ruether, "Christian Anthropology." Certainly Moltmann values mutuality among genders; the question is whether his understanding of the Trinity is an adequate source for reflection on these issues. See also Serene Jones, "This God Which Is Not One."

21. See also Medley, *Imago Trinitas*, 181ff.

22. LaCugna, *God for Us*, 274.

23. For example, Brooks Thistlewaite states, "I would prefer the liberating content of Moltmann's open and inviting understanding of the nature of God as triune, to the seemingly inclusive language which hides a fundamentally oppressive dominance in the Godhead" ("Comments," 182).

24. See Grenz, "Is God Sexual?" for his argument that we cannot locate the feminine in the Spirit because "such compartmentalization is inconsistent with the idea of perichoresis" (36).

The Problematic of *Perichoresis* as Social Norm

In Moltmann's designation of creation as differentiated rupture, ontological fault-lines—if not evil—are built into creation's story with the concomitant need for God's eschatological contradiction of creational difference in redemption. This is true even if the enactment of evil is contingent. The unity of divine life, in the end, stands over against the difference of creaturely life.

In revealing himself as the divine community, God makes the future exist within godforsaken creation. Here the *perichoresis* that is the "mutual indwelling" which results from "self-giving" of each member of the Trinity becomes the norm of all social relations.

Perichoresis is found in God both *in se* and *ad extra*. Moltmann explains the origin and destiny of the Creator-creation relationship in terms of *perichoresis*. However, Creator-creation *perichoresis* seems more problematic as it must take into account the fundamental difference that allows for the distinction between God and non-God. The very difference that allows God to stand over against the *creatio originalis* is called into question by the call to creation to give itself freely and totally over to the divine community.

And here is a fundamental problem. For in distinction from the Trinity, where otherness is in terms of a fundamental likeness, in interhuman relations we face that which is fundamentally unlike. Creaturely *perichoresis* exists under a different set of conditions than that found within inner-trinitarian life. Since mutual indwelling in God presupposes a likeness, the flow of mutuality is between same Others and is characterized by a fail-safe predictability. However, when a human person gives of herself to a different Other, the response of the Other is neither predictable, safe, nor risk free. Rejection and violence are distinct possibilities in a creation characterized by strife and isolation. Nevertheless perichoretic communality demands that I must give myself, even (especially) to the violent Other, for here in lies the chance for redemption.[25] Here hope re-enters the picture. If my giving of self is rejected and destroyed, I still have the promise that God will ultimately overcome all such violence in his fulfillment of creation. The thrust of *perichoresis* is a call for the self's kenosis, a kenosis

---

25. Schuurman questions the very possibility of imitation when he states that "the entire idea of *kenosis* implies an original position of power and rights from which one selflessly descends. Thus it is hard to see what this idea means for one who is not in such a position—namely the poor and oppressed . . . Thus it is not clear what his word of action to the oppressed finally is, based on an ethic of imitation" ("Creation, Eschaton, and Ethics," 59).

in which I constantly give my self over to the creaturely Other and to the divine Other.

In creation, understood as always/already in need of redemption, I don't have many options other than to cease being what I am (forsaken) in order to become Other (filled). In the end, in spite of his real concern for suffering, I am wary of Moltmann making deficiency (and the proclivity for evil) so intrinsic to creation that we are constantly trapped between the horns of sufferings for/from the Other or choosing to be guilty in self assertion.

Reframing *Perichoresis*: A Dance of Beloved Partners

A way of reframing *perichoresis* in order to avoid the downplaying of creation and the related danger of emplanting evil into the fabric of creation has been suggested by Catherine LaCugna in *God for Us*. Rather than locating *perichoresis* in "God's inner life," which makes the economy of redemption the starting point for the discussion of the relationship between God and creation, LaCugna suggestively proposes that we begin "in the mystery of the one communion of all persons, divine as well as human."[26] According to LaCugna, "there are not two sets of communion—one among the divine persons, the Other among human persons, with the latter supposed to replicate the former."[27] Instead, there is "one perochoresis, the one mystery of communion [that] includes God and humanity as beloved partners in the dance."[28] The recognition of the irreducibility of divine and human life and the emphasis on one communion opens the possibility for difference as non-oppositional.[29] Then *perichoresis* can be experienced as an ongoing process of "withing"[30] between God and creation instead of

---

26. LaCugna, *God for Us*, 274. See also Schwöbel's assertion that "the Christian community whose existence is part of the divine economy" (Christology and Trinitarian Thought," 139).

27. Ibid. Plantinga and Feenstra explain that "Moltmann links the two communities—one divine and trinitarian, the other human, but eschatologically progressing toward the divine life—by a soteriology in which the divine creation, sending, passion, and glorification at once mirror the intratrinitarian life and graciously open it to the human community" (*Trinity, Incarnation and Atonement*, 6).

28. Ibid.

29. On this point I think LaCugna is consistent with what Smith calls "incarnational logic" (*Speech and Theology*, 153). For Smith, theology avoids ontotheology by beginning in confession. He maintains the possibility of an "incarnational or analogical account" of theology (ibid.), which, I take, can be extended to the Trinity.

30. For an exploration into the reality of being with an other, see Olthuis, *The Beautiful Risk*.

a simultaneous contradictory process of opposition and interpenetration. Then we have communion as a covenantal dance instead of an alternating opposing/overcoming dialectic exchange between kenosis and theosis, *agape* and *philia*.

Ethics in a Fallen World

Even with a reframing of *perichoresis*, the questions regarding Moltmann's ethics will not have been answered. Although Moltmann, as we have seen, considers self-sacrifice the ethical norm, we also noticed that he allows room for the exercise of self-assertive power in an act of self-protection, which can be called a "choosing to be guilty." This is in tension with and even contradicts the whole direction of his ethics. Our question is: does the need to make the exception of "choosing to be guilty" call into question the credibility of Moltmann's project? Or is the call to constant struggle and self-assertion built ontologically into the heart of Moltmann's ethics? In which case, his emphasis on the eschatological need for constant self-surrender and sacrifice is something that involves from the outset its opposite.

I suspect that one could argue either way. Whatever the case, it seems we are left somewhat, if not completely, in the lurch ethically. All we know is that God is going to win out and be all in all. Love is stronger than death. But how this translates into in the pull and press of daily life is surely ambiguous. Any self-sacrifice or suffering we endure will, looked at eschatologically, transform into glory. If this is not eschatological verification of suffering and evil, it certainly has much of that sound and feel.

Moltmann's *zimzum* understanding of creation with its God-forsaken space, *agape*, and kenosis depend upon a cosmogony that defines difference as opposition. For the difference of Otherness ultimately to exist within the divine fellowship would mean opposition within the community. And it is opposition that is exactly what is overcome by God in theosis.

One dimension of Moltmann's understanding of *creatio originalis* in terms of opposition is that the relationship between human beings as creatures is what Olthuis has described as a "basic opposition between closed selves."[31] In Moltmann's words, humanity's disconnection from God and from itself, which followed upon God's disconnection from creation, leaves humanity stuck in "God-forsaken, transient reality" (*TH* 18) where it is isolated, captive, and closed. In Moltmann's world there can only be two possible modes of action; either one self-asserts and oppresses others or one self-sacrifices at the risk of being oppressed. In such a world a person

---

31. Olthuis, "Face-to-Face," 469.

either "exercises power and becomes dominant and independent—that is selfish—or one surrenders and becomes submissive and dependent—that is, selfless."[32]

The ethical direction given by God's revelation of his kenotic nature clearly dictates to the follower of Christ the answer to the question of whether she should be selfish or selfless. The ideal for follower of Christ is a constant self-giving. Hence, to return violence for the sake of self-protection is a wrong option, even though it may be necessary. The ethical ideal is to give (as emptying) yourself to the violent Other so that he may be restored to the community.

In hope, the self is to be sacrificed so that the self's Other is invited into the open community of God and creation.[33] Christ has taught us that the community takes precedence over self-assertion. But such reconciliation comes at the price of losing oneself for the sake of the Other. However, as one loses oneself in God, the follower of Christ finds her "true" self in the perichoretic relations of God. Theosis always supersedes kenosis. The experience of loss is countered by the simultaneous promise of ultimate redemption.[34]

As both faithful followers and God engage in *agape*, they experience the pain of excessive giving by emptying. Humanity endures suffering for the violent Other.[35] God endures suffering for the sake of the very existence of an Other different than himself. In Moltmann's cosmogony, in the end, presence, *perichoresis*, and harmony trump the counter movements of forsakenness, differentiation, and risk.

Trinitarian ethics reflect this guarantee of presence, a being-in-creation as creation-is-in-God. Within this final guarantee of presence, trinitarian life models the redeemed ethical norms of perfect, predictable self-giving and self-receiving. However, as we have already noticed, in the temporality of our life on this earth, this leaves the self with the difficult choice of being too central (self-assertive and guilty) or too marginal (self-sacrificial but ethically obedient).

Questions regarding the use of power, legitimate resistance, and the development of a hierarchy of obligations are not really addressed in trinitarian ethics, and one is left to his or her own devices. After all the

32. Ibid.

33. See Volf, *Exclusion and Embrace*, 299 n. 7.

34. Volf reminds us that the end for Moltmann is not merely the liberation of victims but a community of love (ibid., 104ff.).

35. Wiebe asserts that "the gospel is not a moralistic program of nonviolence" but rather the issue is "the dignity, the personhood, even of the enemy" ("Revolution," 114).

theoretical maneuvering, as David Cunningham has pointed out, the specific implications of Moltmann's trinitarian ethics are hard to draw out as his theological reflection remains "at a fairly high level of abstraction."[36] Moltmann has confessed that his theology is "not so much concerned with correct doctrine but with concrete doctrine" (*HTG* 167). However, the idealism of his ethics seems anything but practical. As Cunningham puts it, "[Moltmann] rarely offers suggestions as to how the theoretical changes he advocates might be brought about in practice."[37]

Conclusion

The intent of this study was to explore Moltmann's contention that the Trinity provides a moral and ethical program. This exploration turned out to be impossible without a thorough analysis of Moltmann's use of *philia* and *agape*. Moltmann's thought is creative and, at points, extremely helpful. His stress on a faithful following of the way of Jesus Christ in an ethics of discipleship is much appreciated. However, in the end, the distinctions he attempts to draw between *philia* and *agape* offer little practical help for the specifics of the ethical life. While Moltmann's discussion of topics such as patriarchy, oppression, poverty, and justice raise important issues and offer some pastoral guidance for the church, the fruit of his investigations into the *perichoresis* of the Trinity as the norm for human relations is less available. Moltmann's theoretical construction of the Trinity with its championing of self-sacrifice, even as it recognizes the need to some time incur the guilt of self-assertion, leaves us in ambiguity. As such, Moltmann's cosmogony in the end disappoints in its ability to give guidance and direction in negotiating the countless dilemmas that are integral to a daily following of Jesus Christ.

---

36. Cunningham, "These Three Are One," 273. McDougall argues that Cunningham's critique points to "Moltmann's failure to develop an adequate doctrine of sin" (*Pilgrimage of Love*, 148). She thinks that by re-working Moltmann's doctrine of sin she can close the "gap" between Moltmann's trinitarian principles and his concrete proposals. However, if it is true that Moltmann implants evil into cosmic history, he cannot avoid a weak doctrine of sin. To adjust his doctrine of sin is to change his cosmology at a foundational point.

37. Ibid., 43.

Bibliography

A. Works by Jürgen Moltmann

"A Christian Declaration on Human Rights." *Reformed World* 34 (1976) 58–72.

"All Things New: Invited to God's Future." *Asbury Theological Journal* 48 (1993) 29–38.

"Am Ende ist alles Gottes: Hat der Glaube an die Hölle ausgedient?" *Evangelische Kommentare* (1996) 542–43.

"Christ in Cosmic Context." In *Christ and Context: The Confrontation between Gospel and Culture*, edited by Hilary D. Regan and Alan J. Torrance with Antony Wood, 180–91. Edinburgh: T. & T. Clark, 1993.

"Christian Theology and its Problems Today." *Reformed World* 32 (1972) 5–16.

"Communities of Faith and Radical Discipleship: An Interview with Jürgen Moltmann." By Miroslav Volf. *Christian Century* 100 (1983) 246–49.

"Covenant or Leviathan? Political Theology for Modern Times." *Scottish Journal of Theology* 47 (1994) 19–41.

Creating a Just Future: The Politics of Peace and the Ethics of Creation in a Threatened World. Translated by John Bowden. London: SCM, 1989.

"Creation and Redemption." In *Creation, Christ, and Culture: Studies in Honour of T. F. Torrance*, edited by Richard W. A. McKinney, 119–34. Edinburgh: T. & T. Clark, 1976.

"Cross, Theology of the." In *A New Dictionary of Christian Theology*, edited by Alan Richardson and John Bowden, 135–37. London: SCM, 1983.

Das Kommen Gottes: Christliche Eschatologie. Gütersloh: Kaiser, 1995.

Der Geist des Lebens: Eine ganzheitliche Pneumatologie. Munich: Kaiser, 1991.

Der gekreuzigte Gott: Das Kreuz Christi als Grund und Kritik christlicher Theologie. Munich: Kaiser, 1972.

Der Weg Jesu Christi: Christologie in messianischen Dimensionen. Munich: Chr. Kaiser, 1989.

"Descent into Hell." Translated by M. Douglas Meeks. *Duke Divinity School Review* 33 (1968) 115–19.

Experiences of God. Translated by Margaret Kohl. Philadelphia: Fortress, 1980.

Experiences in Theology: Ways and Forms of Christian Theology. Translated by Margaret Kohl. London: SCM, 2000.

"*Gerechtigkeit für Opfer und Täter.*" In *In der Geschichte Des dreieinigen Gottes: Beiträge zur trinitarischen Theologie*, 74–89. Munich: Kaiser, 1991.

God for a Secular Society: The Public Relevance of Theology. Translated by Margaret Kohl. London: SCM, 1999.

God in Creation: An Ecological Doctrine of Creation. Translated by Margaret Kohl. London: SCM, 1985.

"God is Unselfish Love." Translated by Marianne M. Martin. In *The Emptying God: A Buddhist-Jewish-Christian Conversation*, edited by John B. Cobb, Jr. and Christopher Ives, 116–24. Faith Meets Faith. Maryknoll, NY: Orbis, 1990.

Gott in der Schöpfung: Ökologische Schöpfungslehre. Munich: Kaiser, 1985.

Heim, S. Mark. *The Depth of Riches: A Trinitarian Theology of Religious Ends*. Grand Rapids: Eerdmans, 2000.

History and the Triune God: Contributions to Trinitarian Theology. Translated by John Bowden. London: SCM, 1991.

"Hope." In *A New Dictionary of Christian Theology*, edited by Alan Richardson and John Bowden, 272. London: SCM, 1983.

"Hope and Confidence: A Conversation with Ernst Bloch." In *Religion, Revolution and the Future*, translated by M. Douglas Meeks, 149–76. New York: Scribner, 1969.

"Hope and History." *Theology Today* 25 (1968) 369–86.

Hope and Planning. Translated by Margaret Clarkson. London: SCM, 1971.

"Hope and Reality: Contradiction and Correspondence, Response to Trevor Hart." In *God Will Be All in All: The Eschatology of Jürgen Moltmann*, edited by Richard Bauckham, 77–85. Edinburgh: T. & T. Clark, 1999.

"Hope Beyond Time." *Duke Divinity School Review* 33 (1968) 109–14.

"Hope in the Struggle of the People." *Christianity and Crisis* 37 (1977) 49–55.

Im Ende, der Anfang: Eine kleine Hoffnungslehre. Gütersloh: Gütersloher, 2003.

In der Geschichte des dreieinigen Gottes: Beiträge zur trinitarischen Theologie. Munich: Kaiser, 1991.

"In the End, All is God's: Is Belief in Hell Obsolete?" Translated by Paul F. Zahl. *Sewanee Theological Review* 40 (1997) 232–34.

In the End, the Beginning: The Life of Hope. Translated by Margaret Kohl. Minneapolis: Fortress, 2004.

"Jesus and the Kingdom of God." *Asbury Theological Journal* 48 (1993) 5–18.

Jesus Christ for Today's World. Translated by Margaret Kohl. London: SCM, 1994.

Kirche in der Kraft des Geistes: Ein Beitrag zur messianischen Ekklesiologie. Munich: Kaiser, 1975.

"Liberation in the Light of Hope." *Ecumenical Review* 26 (1974) 118–36.

Man: Christian Anthropology in the Conflict of the Present. Translated by John Sturdy. Philadelphia: Fortress, 1974.

On Human Dignity: Political Theology and Ethics. Translated by M. Douglas Meeks. Philadelphia: Fortress, 1984.

"The Passion of Christ and the Suffering of God." *Asbury Theological Journal* 48 (1993) 19–28.

"Perseverance." In *A New Dictionary of Christian Theology*, edited by Alan Richardson and John Bowden, 441–42. London: SCM, 1983.

"Political Theology." *Theology Today* 28 (1971) 5–23.

"Progress and Abyss: Remembering the Future of the Modern World." *Review and Expositor* 97 (2000) 301–14.

Religion, Revolution and the Future. Translated by M. Douglas Meeks. New York: Scribner, 1969.

"Schöpfung im Horizont der Zeit." *Evangelische Theologie* 52 (1992) 86–92.

The Church in the Power of the Spirit: A Contribution to Messianic Ecclesiology. Translated by Margaret Kohl. London: SCM, 1977.

The Coming of God: Christian Eschatology. Translated by Margaret Kohl. Minneapolis: Fortress, 1996.

The Crucified God: The Cross of Christ as the Foundation and Criticism of Christian Theology. Translated by R. A. Wilson and John Bowden. San Francisco: HarperSanFrancisco, 1991.
"The Ecological Crisis: Peace with Nature?" *Scottish Journal of Theology* 9 (1988) 5–18.
"The Expectation of His Coming." *Theology* 88 (1985) 425–28.
The Experiment Hope. Translated by M. Douglas Meeks. Philadelphia: Fortress 1975.
The Future of Creation. Translated by Margaret Kohl. London: SCM, 1979.
The Passion for Life: A Messianic Lifestyle. Translated by M. Douglas Meeks. Philadelphia: Fortress, 1978.
The Power of the Powerless. Translated by Margaret Kohl. London: SCM, 1983.
"The Realism of Hope: The Feast of the Resurrection and the Transformation of the Present Reality." *Concordia Theological Monthly* 40 (1969) 149–55.
"The Revolution of Freedom: The Christian and Marxist Struggle." Translated by M. Douglas Meeks. In *Openings for Marxist-Christian Dialogue*, edited by Thomas W. Ogletree, 47–71. Nashville: Abingdon, 1968.
The Spirit of Life: A Universal Affirmation. Translated by Margaret Kohl. Minneapolis: Fortress, 1992.
The Trinity and the Kingdom: The Doctrine of God. Translated by Margaret Kohl. San Francisco: Harper & Row, 1981.
The Way of Jesus Christ: Christology in Messianic Dimensions. Translated by Margaret Kohl. London: SCM, 1990.
Theologie der Hoffnung: Untersuchungen zu Begründung und zu den Konsequenzen einer christlichen Eschatologie. Munich: Chr. Kaiser, 1966.
Theology and Joy. Translated by Reinhard Ulrich. London: SCM, 1973.
Theology of Hope: On the Ground and the Implications of a Christian Eschatology. Translated by James W. Leitch. London: SCM, 1967.
Theology of Play. Translated by Reinhard Ulrich. New York: Harper & Row, 1972.
"Theology in Germany Today." In *Observations on "The Spiritual Situation of the Age": Contemporary German Perspectives*, edited by Jürgen Habermas, translated by Andrew Buchwalter, 181–205. Studies in Contemporary German Social Thought. Cambridge: MIT Press, 1984.
Theology Today: Two Contributions towards Making Theology Present. Translated by John Bowden. London: SCM, 1988.
Trinität und Reich Gottes: Zur Gotteslehre. Munich: Chr. Kaiser, 1980.
And Hans Kung, eds. *The Ethics of World Religions and Human Rights.* Concilium. London: SCM, 1990.
And Pinchas Lapide. *Jewish Monotheism and Christian Trinitarian Doctrine: A Dialogue.* Translated by Leonard Swidler. Philadelphia: Fortress, 1981.
And M. Douglas Meeks et al. *Hope for the Church: Moltmann in Dialogue with Practical Theology.* Edited and translated by Theodore Runyon. Nashville: Abingdon, 1979.
And Johann-Baptist Metz. *Faith and the Future: Essays on Theology, Solidarity, and Modernity.* Concilium. Maryknoll, NY: Orbis, 1995.
And Elisabeth Moltmann-Wendel. *God—His and Hers.* Translated by John Bowden. New York: Crossroad, 1991.
———. *Humanity in God.* New York: Pilgrim, 1983.
———, et al. *Love: The Foundation of Hope, the Theology of Jürgen Moltmann and Elisabeth Moltmann-Wendel.* Edited by Frederic B. Burnham, Charles S. McCoy and M. Douglas Meeks. San Francisco: Harper & Row, 1988.

———. *Passion for God: Theology in Two Voices*. Louisville: Westminster John Knox, 2003.

And Jürgen Weissbach. *Two Studies in the Theology of Bonhoeffer*. Translated by Reginald H. Fuller and Ilse Fuller. New York: Scribner, 1967.

And Nicholas Wolterstorff, and Ellen T. Charry. *A Passion for God's Reign: Theology, Christian Learning, and the Christian Self*, ed. Miroslav Wolf. Grand Rapids: Eerdmans, 1998.

B. Other Works Consulted

Abbott, D. "Divine Participation and Eschatology in the Theodicies of Paul Tillich and Jürgen Moltmann." Ph.D. diss., University of Virginia, 1987.

Aben, Tersur Akuma. "Moltmann's Social Trinitarianism." Th.M. thesis, Calvin Theological Seminary, 1992.

Ahlers, Rolf "Theory of God and Theological Method." *Dialog* 22 (1983) 235–50.

Althouse, Peter. *Spirit of the Last Days: Pentecostal Eschatology in Conversation with Jürgen Moltmann*. Journal of Pentecostal Theology Supplement Series 25. New York: Sheffield Academic, 2003.

Alves, Rubem A. *A Theology of Human Hope*. New York: Corpus, 1969.

Ansell, Nicholas John. *The Annihilation of Hell: Universal Salvation and the Redemption of Time in the Eschatology of Jürgen Moltmann*. Ph.D. diss., VU University Amsterdam, 2005.

———. "The Call of Wisdom/The Voice of the Serpent: A Canonical Approach to the Tree of Knowledge" *Christian Scholars Review* 31 (2001) 31–58

Asperen, Geertruida Maartje van. *Hope and History: A Critical Inquiry into the Philosophy of Ernst Bloch*. Utrecht: University of Utrecht, 1973.

Attfield, D.G. "Can God be Crucified? A Discussion of J. Moltmann." *Scottish Journal of Theology* 30 (1977) 47–57.

Bauckham, Richard, ed. *God Will Be All in All: The Eschatology of Jürgen Moltmann*. Edinburgh: T. & T. Clark, 1999.

———. "Jürgen Moltmann." In *The Modern Theologians: An Introduction to Christian Theology in the Twentieth Century*, edited by D. F. Ford, 1:293–310. Oxford: Blackwell, 1989.

———. "Jürgen Moltmann's *The Trinity and the Kingdom of God*, and the Question of Pluralism." In *The Trinity in a Pluralistic Age: Theological Essays on Culture and Religion*, edited by Kevin J. Vanhoozer, 155–64. Grand Rapids: Eerdmans, 1997.

———. *Moltmann: Messianic Theology in the Making*. Basingstoke, UK: Pickering, 1987.

———. "Moltmann's *Theology of Hope* Revisited" *Scottish Theological Journal* 42 (1989) 199–214.

———. *The Theology of Jürgen Moltmann*. Edinburgh: T. & T. Clark, 1995.

———. "Theodicy from Ivan Karamazov to Moltmann." *Modern Theology* 4 (1987) 83–97.

———. "Theology after Hiroshima." *Scottish Journal of Theology* 38 (1985) 583–601.

Berkouwer, G. C. *Man: The Image of God*. Translated by Dirk W. Jellema. Grand Rapids: Eerdmans, 1962.

Bloch, Ernst. *A Philosophy of the Future*. Translated by John Cumming. New York: Herder, 1970.

———. *Atheism in Christianity: The Religion of the Exodus and the Kingdom*. Translated by J. T. Swann. New York: Herder, 1972.

———. *The Principle of Hope*. Translated by Neville Plaice et al. 3 vols. Studies in Contemporary German Social Thought. Cambridge: MIT Press, 1986.

Blocher, H. "Immanence and Transcendence in Trinitarian Theology." In *The Trinity in a Pluralistic Age: Theological Essays on Culture and Religion*, edited by Kevin J. Vanhoozer, 104–23. Grand Rapids: Eerdmans, 1997.
Boersma, Hans. *Violence, Hospitality and the Cross: Reappropriating the Atonement Tradition*. Grand Rapids: Baker Academic, 2004.
Boff, Leonardo. *Trinità e società*. Teologia & liberazione. Assisi, Ita.: Citadella, 1987.
Bonhoeffer, Dietrich. *Ethics*. Edited by Eberhard Bethge, translated by Neville Horton Smith. Library of Philosophy and Theology. London: SCM, 1955.
Bouma-Prediger, Steve. *For the Beauty of the Earth: A Christian Vision for Creation Care*. Engaging Culture. Grand Rapids: Baker Academic, 2003.
———. *The Greening of Theology: The Ecological Models of Rosemary Radford Ruether, Joseph Sittler, and Jürgen Moltmann*. AAR Academy 91. Atlanta: Scholars, 1995.
Braaten, C. E. "A Trinitarian Theology of the Cross." *Journal of Religion* 56 (1976) 113–24.
Bracken, Joseph A. *The One in the Many: A Contemporary Reconstruction of the God-World Relationship*. Grand Rapids: Eerdmans, 2001.
Bush, Randall B. *Recent Ideas of Divine Conflict: The Influences of Psychological and Sociological Theories of Conflict Upon the Trinitarian Theology of Paul Tillich and Jürgen Moltmann*. Distinguished Dissertations 9. San Francisco: Mellen Research University Press, 1991.
Caputo, John D. *Against Ethics: Contributions to a Poetics of Obligation with Constant Reference to Deconstruction*. Studies in Continental Thought. Bloomington: Indiana University Press, 1993.
———. *Demythologizing Heidegger*. Indiana Series in the Philosophy of Religion. Bloomington: Indiana University Press, 1993.
———, and Michael Scanlon, editors. *God, the Gift and Postmodernism*. Indiana Series in the Philosophy of Religion. Bloomington: Indiana University Press, 1999.
Chapman, G. Clarke. "Hope and the Ethics of Formation: Moltmann as an Interpreter of Bonhoeffer." *Studies in Religion* 12 (1983) 449–60.
Chopp, Rebecca S. *The Praxis of Suffering: An Interpretation of Liberation and Political Theologies*. Maryknoll, NY: Orbis, 1986.
Cobb, John. B. "Reply to Jürgen Moltmann's 'The Unity of the Triune God.'" *St. Vladimir's Theological Quarterly* 28 (1984) 173–78.
Coffey, David. *Deus Trinitas: the Doctrine of the Triune God*. New York: Oxford University Press, 1999.
Collins, Paul M. *Trinitarian Theology, West and East: Karl Barth, the Cappadocian Fathers, and John Zizioulas*. Oxford: Oxford University Press, 2001.
Conyers, A. J. *God, Hope, and History: Jürgen Moltmann and the Christian Concept of History*. Macon, GA: Mercer University Press, 1988.
Cornelison, R. T. "The Reality of Hope: Moltmann's Vision for Theology." *Asbury Theological Journal* 48 (1993) 109–19.
Cunningham, Conor. *A Genealogy of Nihilism: Philosophies of Nothing and the Difference of Theology*. Radical Orthodoxy. London: Routledge, 2002.
Cunningham, David. *These Three Are One: The Practice of Trinitarian Theology*. Challenges in Contemporary Theology. Malden, MA: Blackwell, 1998.
Dabney, D. Lyle. "The Advent of the Spirit: The Turn to Pneumatology in the Theology of Jürgen Moltmann." *Asbury Theological Journal* 48 (1993) 81–107.
Dalferth, Ingolf U. *Existenz Gottes und christlicher Glaube: Skizzen zu einer eschatologischen Ontologie*. Beiträge zur evangelischen Theologie 93. Munich: Kaiser, 1984.

———. "The Eschatological Roots of the Doctrine of the Trinity." In *Trinitarian Theology Today: Essays on Divine Being and Act*, edited by Christoph Schwöbel, 147–70. Edinburgh: T. & T. Clark, 1995.

Derrida, Jacques. "The Ends of Man." In *After Philosophy: End or Transformation?* edited by Kenneth Baynes et al., 125–58. Cambridge: MIT Press, 1987.

Deuser, Hermann, et al., editors. *Gottes Zukunft-Zukenft der Welt: Festscrift für Jürgen Moltmann zum 60. Geburtstag*. Munich: Kaiser, 1986.

Dillistone, F. W. 'The Theology of Jürgen Moltmann.' *Modern Churchman* 18 (1974–75) 145–50.

Dooyeweerd, H. *A New Critique of Theoretical Thought*. Translated by David H. Freeman and William S. Young. Jordan Station, ON: Paideia, 1984.

Dorrien, Gary J. *Reconstructing the Common Good: Theology and the Social Order*. Maryknoll: Orbis, 1990.

Egmond, A. van. *De Lijdende God in De Britse Theologie van De Negentiende Eeuw*. Amsterdam: VU University Amsterdam, 1986.

Fiddes, Paul S. *The Creative Suffering of God*. Oxford: Clarendon, 1988.

———. *Participating in God: A Pastoral Doctrine of the Trinity*. Louisville: Westminster John Knox, 2000.

Fiorenza, F. P. "Dialectical Theology and Hope." *Heythrop Journal* 9 (1968) 143–63; 10 (1969) 26–42.

Ford, David, ed. *The Modern Theologians: An Introduction to Christian Theology in the Twentieth Century*. 2 vols. Oxford: Blackwell, 1989. Ford, J. C. "Towards an Anthropology of Mutuality: A Critique of Karl Barth's Doctrine of the Male-Female Order as A and B with a Comparison of the Panentheistic Theology of Jürgen Moltmann." Ph.D. diss., Northwestern University, 1984.

French, William. "Returning to Creation: Moltmann's Eschatology Naturalized" *Journal of Religion* 68 (1988) 76–86.

Geertsma, H. G. *Van boven naar voren: Wijsgerige achtergronden en problemen van het theologische denken over geschiedenis bij Jürgen Moltmann*. Kampen, Neth.: Kok, 1980.

Genovesi, V. *Expectant Creativity: The Action of Hope in Christian Ethics*. Washington, DC: University Press of America, 1982.

Gilbertson, Michael. *God and History in the Book of Revelation: New Testament Studies in Dialogue with Pannenberg and Moltmann*. Society for New Testament Studies Monograph Series 124. Cambridge: Cambridge University Press, 2003.

Gilkey, Langdon "The Contribution of Culture to the Reign of God." In *The Future as the Presence of Shared Hope*, edited by Maryellen Muckenhirn, 34–58. New York: Sheed and Ward, 1968.

Goetz, Ronald. "Karl Barth, Jürgen Moltmann, and the Theopaschite Revolution." In *Festschrift: A Tribute to Dr. William Hordern*, edited by Walter Freitag, 17–28. Saskatoon: University of Saskatchewan Press, 1985.

Grenz, Stanley J. "Is God Sexual? Human Embodiment and the Christian Conception of God" *Christian Scholars Review* 28 (1998) 24–41.

———. *Rediscovering the Triune God: The Trinity in Contemporary Theology*. Minneapolis: Fortress, 2004.

———. *The Named God and the Question of Being: A Trinitarian Theo-ontology*. Louisville: Westminster John Knox, 2005.

———. *The Social God and the Relational Self: A Trinitarian Theology of the Imago Dei*. Louisville: Westminster John Knox, 2001.

Gresham, John. "The Social Model of the Trinity and Its Critics" *Scottish Journal of Theology* 46 (1993) 325–40.

———. "The Social Model of the Trinity in the Theologies of Leonard Hodgson, Jürgen Moltmann, and Joseph Bracken." Ph.D. diss., Baylor University, 1991.
Gunton, Colin E. "Christology and Trinitarian Thought." In *Trinitarian Theology Today: Essays on Divine Being and Act*, edited by Chistoph Schwöbel. Edinburgh: T. & T. Clark, 1995.

———. *Father, Son, and Holy Spirit: Essays towards a Fully Trinitarian Theology*. London: T. & T. Clark, 2003.

———. *The One, the Three and the Many: God, Creation, and the Culture of Modernity*. Cambridge: Cambridge University Press, 1993.

———. *The Promise of Trinitarian Theology*. 2nd ed. Edinburgh: T. & T. Clark, 1997.

———. *The Triune Creator: A Historical and Systematic Study*. Grand Rapids: Eerdmans, 1998.

——— and Christoph Schwöbel, eds. *Persons, Divine and Human: King's College Essays in Theological Anthropology*. Edinburgh: T. & T. Clark, 1991.

Gustafson, James M. *Theology and Ethics*. Oxford: Blackwell, 1981.

Hafstad, Kjetil. "Gott in der Natur: Zur Schöpfungslehre Jürgen Moltmann." *Evangelische Theologie* 47 (1987) 460–66.

Hanby, Michael. "Desire: Augustine beyond Western Subjectivity." In *Radical Orthodoxy: A New Theology*, edited by John Milbank et al., 109–26. Radical Orthodoxy. London: Routledge, 1999.

Hauerwas, Stanley. "No Enemy, No Christianity: Theology and Preaching Between the 'Worlds.'" In *The Future of Theology: Essays in Honor of Jürgen Moltmann*, edited by Miroslav Volf et al., 26–34. Grand Rapids: Eerdmans, 1996.

Hays, Richard B. *The Moral Vision of the New Testament: Community, Cross, New Creation, a Contemporary Introduction to New Testament Ethics*. San Francisco: HarperSanFrancisco, 1997.

Heidegger, Martin. "Overcoming Metaphysics." In *The End of Philosophy*, 84–110. Translated by Joan Stambaugh. New York: Harper & Row, 1973.

———. "Theology and Theology." In *The Piety of Thinking: Essays*, translated by James G. Hart and John C. Maraldo, 5–21. Studies in Phenomenology and Existential Philosophy. Bloomington: Indiana University Press, 1976.

Henley, J. "Theology and Human Rights." *Scottish Journal of Theology* 39 (1986) 361–78.

Herman, W. R. "Moltmann's Christology." *Studia Biblica et Theologica* 17 (1989) 3–31.

Herzog, Frederick, editor. *The Future of Hope: Theology as Eschatology*. New York: Herder, 1970.

Hessen, Johannes. *Hegels Trinitätslehre: Zugleich eine Einfürung in Hegels System*. Freiburg: Herder, 1922.

Highfield, Ron. "Divine Self-Limitation in the Theology of Jürgen Moltmann: A Critical Appraisal." *Christian Scholars Review* 22 (2002) 49–71.

Hodgson, Peter C. *Jesus—Word and Presence: An Essay in Christology*. Philadelphia: Fortress, 1971.

Hunsinger, George. "The Crucified God and the Political Theology of Violence." *Heythrop Journal* 14 (1973) 266–79, 379–95.

Irigaray, Luce. *I Love to You: Sketch for a Felicity within History*. Translated by Alison Martin. New York: Routledge, 1996.

Irish, Jerry A. "Moltmann's Theology of Contradiction." *Theology Today* 32 (1975–76) 21–31.

Ising, Dieter, et al. *Bibliographie Jürgen Moltmann*. Munich: Kaiser, 1987.

Jansen, Henry. "Moltmann's View of God's (Im)mutability: The God of the Philosophers and the God of the Bible." *Neue Zeitschrift für systmatische Theologie und Religionsphilosophie* 36 (1994) 284–301.

———. *Relationality and the Concept of God*. Currents of Encounter 10. Amsterdam: Rodopi, 1994.

Jantzen, G. M. "Christian Hope and Jesus' Despair." *King's Theological Review* 5 (1982) 1–7.

Jenson, Robert W. *On Thinking the Human: Resolutions of Difficult Notions*. Grand Rapids: Eerdmans, 2003.

Jones, L. Gregory. *Transformed Judgment: Toward a Trinitarian Account of the Moral Life*. Notre Dame: University of Notre Dame Press, 1990.

Jones, Serene. "This God Which Is Not One: Irigaray and Barth on the Divine." In *Transfigurations: Theology and the French Feminists*, edited by C. W. Maggie Kim et al., 109–42. Minneapolis: Fortress, 1993.

Jüngel, Eberhard. *The Doctrine of the Trinity: God's being Is in Becoming*. Translated by Horton Harris. Grand Rapids: Eerdmans, 1976.

———. *God as the Mystery of the World: On the Foundation of the Theology of the Crucified One, in the Dispute between Theism and Atheism*. Translated by Darrell L. Guder. Grand Rapids: Eerdmans, 1983.

Kearney, Richard. "Desire of God." In *God, the Gift and Postmodernism*, edited by John D. Caputo and Michael Scanlon, 112–29. Indiana Series in the Philosophy of Religion. Bloomington: Indiana University Press, 1999.

———. *The God Who May Be: A Hermeneutics of Religion*. Indiana Series in the Philosophy of Religion. Bloomington: Indiana University Press, 2001.

Klappert, B. "Christologie in messianischen Dimensionen: J. Moltmanns Buch 'Der Weg Jesu Christi.'" *Evangelische Theologie* 50 (1990) 574–86.

Klapwijk, Jacob, et al., editors. *Bringing into Captivity Every Thought: Capita Selecta in the History of Christian Evaluations of Non-Christian Philosophy*. Lanham, MD: University Press of America, 1991.

Kristeva, Julia. *Tales of Love*. Translated by Leon S. Roudiez. New York: Columbia University Press, 1987.

Kuratmatsu, Isao. "Die gegenwörtige Kreuzestheologie und Luther, besonders in Rücksicht auf die Theologie des Schmerzes Gottes von Kazo Kitamori." *Kerygma und Dogma* 36 (1990) 273–83.

LaCugna, Catherine Mowry. *God for Us: The Trinity and Christian Life*. San Francisco: HarperSanFrancisco, 1991.

Levering, Matthew Webb. *Scripture and Metaphysics: Aquinas and the Renewal of Trinitarian Theology*. Challenges in Contemporary Theology. Malden, MA: Blackwell, 2004.

Lévinas, Emmanuel. "Ethics of the Infinite." In *Debates in Continental Philosophy: Conversation with Contemporary Thinkers*, edited by Richard Kearney, 13–33. Perspectives in Continental Philosophy 37. New York: Fordham University Press, 2004.

———. *Of God Who Comes to Mind*. Translated by Bettina Bergo. Meridian: Crossing Aesthetics. Stanford: Stanford University Press, 1998.

———. and Richard Kearney. "Dialogue with Emmanuel Lévinas." In *Face to Face with Lévinas*, edited by Richard A. Cohen, 13–34. SUNY Series in Philosophy. Albany: SUNY Press, 1986.

Loeschen, John R. *The Divine Community: Trinity, Church, and Ethics in Reformation Theologies*. Sixteenth Century Texts and Studies 1. Kirksville, MO: Sixteenth Century Journal Publishers, 1981.

Lønning, Per. "Die Schöpfungstheologie Jürgen Moltmanns—Eine nordische Perspektive." *Kerygma und Dogma* 33 (1987) 207–23.

Lowe, Walter. *Theology and Difference: The Wound of Reason*. Indiana Series in the Philosophy of Religion. Bloomington: Indiana University Press, 1993.

Lunn, A. J. "The Doctrine of Atonement: The Significance of the Cross for Moltmann and Dillistone. " *Epworth Review* 19 (1992) 26–34.

MacDade, J. "The Trinity and the Paschal Mystery." *Heythrop Journal* 29 (1988) 175–91.

Mackey, James Patrick. *The Christian Experience of God as Trinity*. London: SCM, 1983.

MacPherson, J. "Life, the Universe and Everything: Jürgen Moltmann's *God's in Creation*." *St. Mark's Review* 128 (1986) 34–46.

Marion, Jean-Luc. *God Without Being: Hors-Texte*. Translated by Thomas Carlson. Religion and Postmodernism. Chicago: University of Chicago Press, 1991.

———. "In the Name: How to Avoid Speaking of 'Negative Theology.'" In *God, the Gift and Postmodernism*, edited by John D. Caputo and Michael Scanlon, 20–53. Indiana Series in the Philosophy of Religion. Bloomington: Indiana University Press, 1999.

Mason, G. "God's Freedom as Faithfulness: A Critique of Jürgen Moltmann's Social Trinitarianism." Ph.D. diss., Southwestern Baptist Theological Seminary, 1987.

Matić, Marko. *Jürgen Moltmanns Theologie in Auseinandersetzung mit Ernst Bloch*. Europäische Hochschulschriften 23/209. Frankfurt: Lang, 1983.

McDougall, Joy Ann. *Pilgrimage of Love: Moltmann on the Trinity and Christian Life*. Reflection and Theory in the Study of Religion. Oxford: Oxford University Press, 2005.

McWilliams, W. "Divine Suffering in Contemporary Theology." *Scottish Journal of Theology* 33 (1980) 35–53.

———. *The Passion of God: Divine Suffering in Contemporary Protestant Theology*. Macon, GA: Mercer University Press, 1985.

Medley, Mark S. *Imago Trinitas: Toward a Relational Understanding of Becoming Human*. Lanham, MD: UPA, 2002.

Meeks, M. Douglas. *Origins of the Theology of Hope*. Philadelphia: Fortress, 1974.

———. "The Future of Theology in a Commodity Society." In *The Future of Theology: Essays in Honor of Jürgen Moltmann*, edited by Miroslav Volf et al, 253–66. Grand Rapids: Eerdmans, 1996.

Metz, J. B. "Suffering unto God." *Critical Inquiry* 20 (1994) 611–23.

Meyendorff, John. *A Study of Gregory Palamas*. Translated by George Lawrence. Crestwood, NY: St. Vladimir's Seminary Press, 1998.

———. "Reply to Jürgen Moltmann's 'The Unity of the Triune God.'" *St. Vladimir's Theological Quarterly* 28 (1984) 183–88.

Migliore, D. L. "Biblical Eschatology and Political Hermeneutics." *Theology Today* 26 (1969–70) 116–32.

Míguez-Bonino, José. *Revolutionary Theology Comes of Age*. London: SPCK, 1975.

Milbank, John. "Can Morality Be Christian?" *Studies in Christian Ethics* 8 (1995) 45–59.

———. "The Second Difference." *Modern Theology* 2 (1986) 213–34.

———. *The Word Made Strange: Theology, Language, and Culture*. Cambridge: Blackwell, 1997.

———, Catherine Pickstock, and Graham Ward, eds. *Radical Orthodoxy: A New Theology*. Radical Orthodoxy. London: Routledge, 1999.

Molnar, Paul. "The Function of the Immanent Trinity in the Theology of Karl Barth: Implications for Today." *Scottish Journal of Theology* 42 (1989) 367–99.

———. "The Function of the Trinity in Moltmann's Ecological Doctrine of Creation." *Theological Studies* 51 (1990) 673–97.

Bibliography

Momoze, P. F. *Kreuzetheologie: Eine Auseinanderseztung mit Jürgen Moltmann. Mit einem Nachwort von Jürgen Moltmann.* Freiburg: Herder, 1978.

Morse, Christopher. *The Logic of Promise in Moltmann's Theology.* Philadelphia: Fortress, 1979.

Mortensen, Viggo. "Schöpfungstheologie und Anthropologie." *Evangelische Theologie* 47 (1987) 466–72.

Muckenhirn, Maryellen, ed., *The Future as the Presence of Shared Hope.* New York: Sheed and Ward, 1968.

Mueller, David. L. *Foundation of Karl Barth's Doctrine of Reconciliation: Jesus Christ Crucified and Risen.* Toronto Studies in Theology 54. Lewiston, NY: Mellen, 1990.

Muller, R.A. 'Christ in the Eschaton: Calvin and Moltmann on the Duration of the Munus Regium.' *Harvard Theological Review* 74 (1981) 31–59.

Müller-Fahrenholz, Geiko. *The Kingdom and the Power: The Theology of Jürgen Moltmann.* Translated by John Bowden. London: SCM, 2000.

Neuhaus, Richard John. "Moltmann vs. Monotheism." *Dialog* 20 (1981) 239–43.

Niewiadomski, Józef. *Die Zweideutigkeit von Gott und Welt in J. Moltmanns Theologien.* Innsbrucker theologische Studien 9. Innsbruck, Austria: Tyrolia, 1982.

Nygren, Anders. *Agape and Eros.* Translated by Philip S. Watson. Chicago: University of Chicago Press, 1982. First published 1953 by Westminster Press.

O'Collins, Gerald. *The Tripersonal God: Understanding and Interpreting the Trinity.* New York: Paulist, 1999.

O'Donnell, John J. "The Doctrine of the Trinity in Recent German Theology." *Heythrop Journal* 23 (1982) 153–67.

———. "The Trinity as Divine Community: A Critical Reflection upon Recent Theological Developments." *Gregorianum* 69 (1988) 5–34.

———. *Trinity and Temporality: The Christian Doctrine of God in the Light of Process Theology and the Theology of Hope.* Oxford Theological Monographs. Oxford: Oxford University Press, 1983.

Oliver, Kelly. *Reading Kristeva: Unraveling the Double-bind.* Bloomington: Indiana University Press, 1993.

Olson, Roger E. *The Story of Christian Theology: Twenty Centuries of Tradition & Reform.* Downers Grove, IL: InterVarsity, 1999.

———. "Trinity and Eschatology: The Historical Being of God in Jürgen Moltmann and Wolfhart Pannenberg." *Scottish Journal of Theology* 36 (1983) 213–27.

———. and Christopher A. Hall. *The Trinity.* Guides to Theology. Grand Rapids: Eerdmans, 2002.

Olthuis, James H. "A Cold and Comfortless Hermeneutic or a Warm and Trembling Hermeneutic: A Conversation with John D. Caputo." *Christian Scholars Review* 19 (1990) 345–62.

———. "A Radical Ontology of Love: Thinking 'with' Radical Orthodoxy." In *Radical Orthodoxy and the Reformed Tradition: Creation, Covenant, and Participation,* edited by James H. Olthuis and James K. A. Smith. Grand Rapids: Baker Academic, 2005.

———. "Be(com)ing: Humankind as Gift and Call." *Philosophia Reformata* 58 (1993) 153–72.

———. "Face-to-Face: Ethical Asymmetry or the Symmetry of Mutuality?" *Studies in Religion/Sciences Religieuses* 25 (1996) 459–79.

———. "God as True Infinite: Concerns about Pannenberg's *Systematic Theology, Vol. 1.*" *Calvin Theological Journal* 27 (1992) 318–25.

———. *Models of Humankind in Theology and Psychology.* Rev. ed. Toronto: ICS, 1990.

———. "Otherwise than Violence: Towards a Hermeneutics of Connection." In *The Arts, Community, and Cultural Democracy*, edited by Lambert Zuidervaart and Henry Luttikhuizen, 137–64. Cross-Currents in Religion and Culture. New York: St. Martin's, 2000.

———. *The Beautiful Risk: A New Psychology of Loving and Being Loved*. Grand Rapids: Zondervan, 2001.

———. and James K. A. Smith, eds. *Radical Orthodoxy and the Reformed Tradition: Creation, Covenant, and Participation*. Grand Rapids: Baker Academic, 2005.

Otto, Randall E. "God and History in Jürgen Moltmann." *Journal of Evangelical Theology* 35 (1992) 81–90.

———. "The Eschatological Nature of Moltmann's Theology." *Westminster Theological Journal* 54 (1992) 115–33.

———. *The God of Hope: The Trintarian Vision of Jürgen Moltmann*. Lanham, MD: UPA, 1991.

Pannenberg, Wolfhart. *An Introduction to Systematic Theology*. Grand Rapids: Eerdmans, 1991.

———. *Anthropology in Theological Perspective*. Translated by Matthew J. O'Connell. Philadelphia: Westminster, 1985.

———. *Basic Questions in Theology*. Translated by George H. Kehm. Vols. 1–2. Philadelphia: Westminster, 1983.

———. *Human Nature, Election, and History*. Philadelphia: Westminster, 1977.

———. *Metaphysics and the Idea of God*. Translated by Philip Clayton. Grand Rapids: Eerdmans, 1990.

———. *Systematic Theology*. Translated by Geoffrey W. Bromiley. 3 vols. Grand Rapids: Eerdmans, 1991–98.

———. *Theology and the Kingdom of God*. Philadelphia: Westminster, 1969.

Peters, Ted. *God as Trinity: Relationality and Temporality in the Divine Life*. Louisville: Westminster/John Knox, 1993.

———. "Moltmann and the Way of the Trinity." *Dialog* 31 (1992) 272–79.

———. "Trinity Talk: Part I" *Dialog* 26 (1987) 44–47.

Phillips, Steven. "The Use of Scripture in Liberation Theologies: An Examination of Juan Luis Segundo, James H. Cone, and Jürgen Moltmann." Ph.D. diss., Southern Baptist Theological Seminary, 1978.

Plantinga, Cornelius, Jr., and Ronald J. Feenstra, eds. *Trinity, Incarnation, and Atonement: Philosophical and Theological Essays*. Library of Religious Philosophy 1. Notre Dame: University of Notre Dame Press, 1989.

Powell, Samuel M. *The Trinity in German Thought*. Cambridge: Cambridge University Press, 2001.

Prokes, Mary Timothy. *Mutuality: The Human Image of Trinitarian Love*. New York: Paulist, 1993.

Rasmusson, Arne. *The Church as Polis: From Political Theology to Theological Politics as Exemplified by Jürgen Moltmann and Stanley Hauerwas*. Notre Dame: University of Notre Dame Press, 1995.

Ricoeur, Paul. *Oneself as Another*. Translated by Kathleen Blamey. Chicago: University of Chicago Press, 1992.

———. "The Golden Rule: Exegetical and Theological Perplexities." *New Testament Studies* 36 (1990) 392–97.

Rogers, Eugene F. *Sexuality and the Christian Body: Their Way into the Triune God*. Challenges in Contemporary Theology. Malden, MA: Blackwell, 1999.

Rouner, Leroy. S., ed. *On Community*. Boston University Studies in Philosophy and Religion 12. Notre Dame: University of Notre Dame Press, 1991.
Ruether, Rosemary Radford. "Christian Anthropology and Gender: A Tribute to Jürgen Moltmann." In *The Future of Theology: Essays in Honor of Jürgen Moltmann*, edited by Miroslav Volf et al, 241–52. Grand Rapids: Eerdmans, 1996.
Rusch, William, ed. *The Trinitarian Controversy*. Sources of Early Christian Thought. Philadelphia: Fortress, 1980.
Sarot, Marcel. "Het Lijden Van God?" *Nederlands Theologisch Tildschift* 44 (1990) 35–50.
Schuurman, Douglas James. "Creation, Eschaton and Ethics: An Analysis of Theology and Ethics in Jürgen Moltmann." *Calvin Theological Journal* 22 (1987) 42–67.
———. *Creation, Eschaton, and Ethics: The Ethical Significance of Creation-Eschaton Relation in the Thought of Emil Brunner and Jürgen Moltmann*. American University Studies VII. Theology and Religion 86. New York: Lang, 1991.
Schwöbel, Chistoph, ed. *Trinitarian Theology Today: Essays on Divine Being and Act*. Edinburgh: T. & T. Clark, 1995.
Seerveld, Calvin. "Biblical Wisdom Underneath Vollenhoven's Categories for Philosophical Historiography." In *The Idea of a Christian Philosophy: Essays in Honor of D. H. Th. Vollenhoven*, edited by K. A. Bril, et al. Toronto: Wedge Publishing Foundation, 1973.
Smith, James K. A. *Speech and Theology: Language and the Logic of Incarnation*. London: Routledge, 2002.
Soble, Alan, ed. *Eros, Agape and Philia: Readings in the Philosophy of Love*. New York: Paragon, 1989.
Sponheim, Paul R. *Faith and the Other: A Relational Theology*. Minneapolis: Fortress, 1993.
Taylor, Mark K. "Denegating God." *Critical Inquiry* 20 (1994) 592–610.
Thévenaz, Jean-Pierre. "Le Dieu crucifié a-t-il une histoire?" *Revue de Théologie et de Philosophie* 115 (1983) 199–208.
Thistlewaite, Susan Brooks. "Comments on Jürgen Moltmann's 'The Unity of the Triune God.'" *St. Vladimirs Theological Quarterly* 28 (1984) 179–84.
Thompson, John. *Modern Trinitarian Perspectives*. New York: Oxford University Press, 1994.
Torrance, T. F. *The Christian Doctrine of God, One Being Three Persons*. Edinburgh: T. & T. Clark, 1996.
Turcescu, Lucian. *Gregory of Nyssa and the Concept of Divine Persons*. AAR Academy Series. Oxford: Oxford University Press, 2005.
Valk, John. "The Concept of *Coincidentia Oppositorium* in the Thought of Mircea Eliade." M.Phil. thesis, Institute for Christian Studies, 1977.
Volf, Miroslav. "A Queen and a Beggar: Challenges and Prospects in Theology." In *The Future of Theology: Essays in Honor of Jürgen Moltmann*, edited by Miroslav Volf et al, ix–xviii. Grand Rapids: Eerdmans, 1996.
———. *After Our Likeness: The Church as the Image of the Trinity*. Sacra Doctrina. Grand Rapids: Eerdmans, 1998.
———. "Eschaton, Creation, and Social Ethics." *Calvin Theological Journal* 30 (1995) 130–43.
———. *Exclusion and Embrace: A Theological Exploration of Identity, Otherness and Reconciliation*. Nashville: Abingdon, 1996.
———. "The Trinity Is Our Social Program." *Modern Theology* 14 (1998) 403–23.
Vollenhoven, D. H. T. 'De Consequent Probleemhistoriche Methode." *Philosophia Reformata* 26 (1961) 1–34.

Wakefield, James L. *Jürgen Moltmann: A Research Bibliography*. ATLA Bibliography 47. Lanham, MD: Scarecrow, 2002.
Walsh, Brian. "Pannenberg's Eschatological Ontology." *Christian Scholar's Review* 15 (1982) 229–42.
———. "Theology of Hope and the Doctrine of Creation: An Appraisal of Jürgen Moltmann." *Evangelical Quarterly* 59 (1987) 53–76.
———. Review of *The Trinity and the Kingdom of God*, by Jürgen Moltmann in *Christian Scholar's Review* 12.3 (1984).
Ward, Graham. "The Revelation of the Holy Other as Wholly Other. Between Barth's Theology of Word and Levinas' Philosophy of Saying." *Modern Theology* 9 (1993) 159–80.
Ward, Keith. *Religion and Creation*. Oxford: Clarendon, 1996.
Webb, Stephen H. *The Gifting God: A Trinitarian Ethics of Excess*. New York: Oxford University Press, 1996.
Webster, J. B. *Barth's Moral Theology: Human Action in Barth's Thought*. Edinburgh: T. & T. Clark, 1998.
Welker, Michael, ed. *Diskussion über Jürgen Moltmanns "Buch Der Gekreuzigte Gott."* Munich: Kaiser, 1979.
West, Philip. "Cruciform Labour? The Cross in Two Recent Theologies of Work." *Modern Churchman* 28 (1986) 9–15.
Westphal, Merold. "Overcoming Onto-theology." In *God, the Gift and Postmodernism*, edited by John D. Caputo and Michael Scanlon, 146–69. Indiana Series in the Philosophy of Religion. Bloomington: Indiana University Press, 1999.
Wiebe, Ben. "Revolution as an Issue in Theology: Jürgen Moltmann" *Restoration Quarterly* 26 (1983) 105–20.
Williams, Rowan. "The Philosophical Structures of Palamism." *Eastern Churches Review* 9 (1977) 27–44.
Willis, W. Waite. *Theism, Atheism and the Doctrine of the Trinity: The Trinitarian Theologies of Karl Barth and Jürgen Moltmann in response to Protest Atheism*. AAR Academy Series 53. Atlanta: Scholars, 1987.
Wolters, Albert. "On Vollenhoven's Problem-Historical Method." In *Hearing and Doing: Philosophical Essays Dedicated to H. Evan Runner*, edited by John Kraay and Anthony Tol, 231–62. Toronto: Wedge, 1979.
Wood, Laurence. "From Barth's Trinitarian Christology to Moltmann's Trinitarian Pneumatology: A Methodist Perspective." *Asbury Theological Journal* 48 (1993) 49–79.
Wright, N. T. *Jesus and the Victory of God*. Christian Origins and the Question of God 2. Minneapolis: Fortress, 1996.
Wright, Nigel. *Disavowing Constantine: Mission, Church and the Social Order in the Theologies of John Howard Yoder and Jürgen Moltmann*. Paternoster Biblical and Theological Monographs. Carlisle, UK: Paternoster, 2000.
Wyschogrod, Edith. *Saints and Postmodernism: Revisioning Moral Philosophy*. Religion and Postmodernism. Chicago: University of Chicago Press, 1990.
Yoo, Tae Wha. *The Spirit of Liberation: Jürgen Moltmann's Trinitarian Pneumatology*. Studies in Reformed Theology, Supplements 2. Zoetermeer, Neth.: Meinema, 2003.
Zizioulas, John. *Being as Communion: Studies in Personhood and the Church*. Contemporary Greek theologians 4. Crestwood, NY: St. Vladimir's Seminary Press, 1985.
———. "The Doctrine of the Holy Trinity." In *Trinitarian Theology Today: Essays on Divine Being and Act*, edited by Christoph Schwöbel, 44–60. Edinburgh: T. & T. Clark, 1995.

www.ingramcontent.com/pod-product-compliance
Lightning Source LLC
Chambersburg PA
CBHW070915160426
43193CB00011B/1461